New Headway

Advanced

Teacher's Resource Book

Jayne Wildman

John and Liz Soars

OXFORD

UNIVERSITY PRESS

OXFORD
UNIVERSITY PRESS

Great Clarendon Street, Oxford OX2 6DP

Oxford University Press is a department of the University of Oxford.
It furthers the University's objective of excellence in research, scholarship,
and education by publishing worldwide in

Oxford New York

Auckland Bangkok Buenos Aires Cape Town Chennai
Dar es Salaam Delhi Hong Kong Istanbul Karachi Kolkata
Kuala Lumpur Madrid Melbourne Mexico City Mumbai
Nairobi São Paulo Shanghai Taipei Tokyo Toronto

OXFORD and OXFORD ENGLISH are registered trade marks of
Oxford University Press in the UK and in certain other countries

ACKNOWLEDGEMENTS

Illustrations by: Jeremy Banx pp23, 53; Mark Duffin p25; Harry Venning
pp17, 71, 74

We would also like to thank the following for permission to reproduce photographs:
Action-Plus pp55 (PhotoNews/DPPI/cyclists), (G.Kirk/footballers), 61 (B.van
Loocke/DPPI/sand skiing); Alamy p55 (firemen and truck), (policemen and
boy), (soldier and civilian); Getty Digital Vision p67; Getty PhotoDisc Blue
p55; Getty PhotoDisc Green p33; Phil Shaw/www.extremeironing.com p61
(underwater ironing)

*The authors and publisher are grateful to those who have given permission to
reproduce the following extracts and adaptations of copyright material*: p11 'Doh!
Rio blames it on The Simpsons' by Alex Bellos, The Guardian Tuesday 9
April 2002 © Alex Bellos. Reproduced by permission; p39 'Man stuck in
chimney says he was chasing his parrot' from www.ananova.com.
Reproduced by permission; p39 'Man builds gun to fire pumpkin a mile'
from www.ananova.com. Reproduced by permission; p39 'Dogs to be used
to advertise' from www.ananova.com. Reproduced by permission; p39
'Missing teenager lived on chewing gum during ordeal' from
www.ananova.com. Reproduced by permission; p46–47 'Allison has twice
woken up on a mortuary slab. Now her biggest fear is being buried alive'
by Julia Llewellyn Smith, The Express Tuesday 17 October 2000.
Reproduced by permission of Express Newspapers; p46–47 'Edwin
Robinson suffered a severe head injury …' from www.forteantimes.com.
Reproduced by permission; p46–47 'On 5 November 1975, a forestry
worker called Travis Walton …' from www.forteantimes.com. Reproduced
by permission; p46–47 'A crowd of 50 in Keithville, Lousiana …' from
www.forteantimes.com. Reproduced by permission; p61 Information about
the International Olympic Committee. Reproduced by permission

Introduction

This Teacher's Resource Book contains thirty-seven photocopiable activities and further ideas for you to use with *New Headway Advanced*. It is a completely new component for the *Headway* series and has been written with two aims in mind:

- to give teachers additional material that revises and extends the work in the Student's Book

- to give students lots of extra speaking practice!

Students at advanced level need lots of opportunities to 'get active' and actually use their English in meaningful and relevant contexts. The activities in this book are designed to help your students do this. They encourage students to talk about themselves, compare opinions and views about the world, and practise the kind of situations they are likely to encounter in real life.

In addition, every activity involves an element of team work. Students will need to work together to share or check information, and agree outcomes or solutions. In other words, every activity encourages purposeful interaction where students need to speak and listen to each other.

Through role plays, language games, questionnaires, and information gap activities, students are also given the chance to build their confidence and introduce a more personal dimension to their learning.

How to use the photocopiable activities

Each activity starts with the following information:

Aim	The main focus of the activity
Language	The grammar/function/vocabulary exploited
Skills	Speaking, Reading, Writing, and/or Listening
Materials	Notes for preparation of worksheet

Pre-activity

These activities act as a warm-up before the students carry out the main activity. They act to remind the students of the necessary language needed and to set the context. They are optional, particularly if you are following straight on from the corresponding lesson in the Student's Book.

Procedure

This section has step-by-step instructions for carrying out the main activity. Each main activity takes between fifteen and forty-five minutes and is suitable for most class sizes. (There are additional notes for larger classes.) For each activity there is a photocopiable worksheet. Some of the worksheets need to be cut up before handing out to students.

Extension

After each main activity, there is a suggestion for an extension activity. These are generally writing activities which build on the language or topics covered in the main activity. Where this is the case, they can be assigned for homework.

Contents

Worksheet	Description	Language
7.1 Graffiti wisdom	Matching halves of graffiti quotations	Fluency practice
7.2 Strange, but true	Reading short strange stories and speculating about possible explanations	Modals to express past possibility and certainty
7.3 Two points of view	Discussing problem letters sent to an agony aunt and offering advice	Giving advice
8.1 Going round in circles	Playing a card game making metaphors and idioms	Metaphors and idioms
8.2 I wish …	Playing a board game to talk about wishes and regrets or improbable situations	Wishes and regrets; Improbable situations
8.3 Picture this	Describing pictures, then writing a dialogue	Speculating; Wishes and regrets; Fluency practice
9.1 The same, but different	Playing a game identifying words with the same spelling but different pronunciation and meanings	Homographs; Giving definitions
9.2 Place your bets	Identifying and correcting grammatical mistakes	Verb patterns
10.1 But is it a sport?	Defining sport, then choosing two sports to be included in the next Olympic games	Fluency practice
10.2 Personality quiz	Writing options for some questions and the personality profile for a personality quiz	Character adjectives; Intensifying adverbs; Giving advice
10.3 Body language	Practising expressions with parts of the body words	Expressions with parts of the body words in noun and verb form, e.g. *thumb a lift, be all fingers and thumbs*
10.4 Sports reports	Interviewing someone to find factual discrepancies between two newspaper stories	Asking and answering questions
11.1 Holiday clinic	Discussing and agreeing on the best holiday for a group of friends	Suggesting; Agreeing and disagreeing
11.2 Where in the world?	Describing and identifying a holiday destination	Compound nouns and adjectives to talk about the weather and places
11.3 A tale of two cities	Putting a story in order, then retelling it using participle clauses	Present participles
12.1 Time flies …	Completing sentences with expressions with *time*, then making a domino chain with the sentences	Expressions with *time*; Fluency practice
12.2 Time capsule	Selecting the contents for a time capsule	Making suggestions; Giving reasons
12.3 Race against time! 2	Quiz to revise grammar and vocabulary from Units 7–12	Grammar and vocabulary review

1.1

A place to live

Aim	

Aim

To decide which city people would like to live and work in

Language

Expressing a preference
Making suggestions

Skills

Reading, Listening, and Speaking

Lesson link

Use after Unit 1, SB p8, 9, 10 & 11

Materials

One copy of the worksheet cut up per group of four students

Pre-activity (10 minutes)

- Brainstorm with students reasons why people move to different cities or countries (e.g. for a job, to study, immigration, as refugees, for a better standard of living).
- Brainstorm different factors which determine quality of life in a new place (e.g. cost of living, health care, crime rate, public transport and leisure facilities, cultural barrier, environmental cleanliness, food, the weather, language barrier).

Procedure (30 minutes)

- Explain that students have been offered a job by an international company which has offices in cities around the world. They are going to talk to the company's Human Resources department about the best location for them and their family.
- Divide students into an even number of pairs: A and B. (If you have an odd number of pairs, make two groups of three.) Explain that Pairs A are Helen (who has been offered the job) and her husband, Greg, and Pairs B are the Human Resources managers who are going to help them make their choice. Give Pairs A worksheet A, and Pairs B worksheet B.
- Give students time to read their roles, look at the useful language, check any items of vocabulary, and brainstorm questions or criteria with their partner. Go around helping with vocabulary as necessary. Tell students that they will be given information about the choice of cities later on.
- When everybody is ready, make groups of four with a Pair A and a Pair B. Give each group a copy of Worksheet C. Explain that the scores for the cost of living and environmental cleanliness are based on New York, which was used as an average and given 100 in each category.
- Students are now ready to have their meeting. Using the city information in Worksheet C, students discuss and choose the best city. The Human Resources managers ask questions and then make suggestions. Helen and Greg talk about their preferences and try to come to a decision. Go around listening, helping as necessary.
- Have a class feedback session. Ask groups to tell the class Helen and Greg's choice of destination and to explain their reasons.

Extension (10 minutes)

- Ask students, in pairs, to think about the advantages and disadvantages of living in the city they are in now, or one they know well. Ask them to write an email to a friend who is considering moving there, giving them information they might find useful. Go around helping with vocabulary as necessary.

A

Helen and Greg

Helen, you have been offered a job by an international company which has offices in cities around the world. You are going to talk to the Human Resources managers about the best location for you and your family – you are married to Greg and you have two teenage children. Before you have the meeting, read the information below with Greg, then brainstorm the criteria for your ideal destination.

> **HELEN** You would like to live in a city which is medium-sized and safe. You would prefer a place with a low cost of living as you want to be able to send your children to private school. Your favourite pastimes are going to the cinema or reading a good book. You're not interested in outdoor sports and would like to live in a warm climate.

> **GREG** You would like to live a city which is big and exciting, with plenty of job opportunities. You have recently lost your job as a consultant and are looking for a new position. You would prefer a place with a low cost of living, although if you manage to find a job this won't be so important. Your favourite pastimes are outdoor sports, especially skiing. You would   prefer to live in a cold climate. You can speak several European languages.

Now you are ready to talk to the Human Resources managers. Be prepared to answer their questions and to express your preferences. Here is some useful language to help you.

- If I had the choice, I'd …
- I think it'd be better to …
- I'm not really bothered about …, so …
- I'd definitely choose/prefer to …

B

Human Resources managers

You work for an international company based in London. It's a fast-expanding company with new offices and job opportunities all over the world. Your job is to match new employees and their families to locations which best suit their needs. Use these prompts to brainstorm questions you will need to ask them. Add some of your own questions.

> **FAMILY SITUATION**
> - children?
> - spouse working or not?
>
> **GENERAL**
> - languages?
> - prefer hot/cold climate?
> - location?
> - cost of living?
> - free time activities?

Now you are ready to talk to Helen and her husband, Greg. Once you have asked your questions and listened to their preferences, be prepared to make suggestions. Here is some useful language to help you.

- Have you looked at + -ing/noun?
- What about + -ing?
- Would you consider …?
- It seems to me that the best place for you would be …

C

	Cost of living	Environmental cleanliness	Population	Average temperature	Extra information
NEW YORK	100	100	16.6 million	Jan: -3 – 3 Aug: 20 – 28	Medium crime rate, excellent recreational facilities (i.e. cinemas, theatre, sport, restaurants)
MEXICO CITY	80.8	29.5	18.2 million	Jan: 7 – 21 Aug: 12 – 23	The biggest metropolis in the world, high crime rate, high poverty, fair recreational facilities
ZURICH	79.8	149.5	484,000	Jan: -2 – 2 Aug: 12 – 21	On Lake Zurich near the mountains, low crime rate, excellent outdoor sports
WARSAW	74.6	103	1.6 million	Jan: -5 – 0 Aug: 12 – 23	City divided into historic part and industrial part, fair recreational facilities, medium crime rate
JOHANNESBURG	34.4	128	2.5 million	Jan: 11 – 30 Aug: 0 – 24	High crime rate, high unemployment, poverty, fair recreational facilities
SYDNEY	58.4	124	4.2 million	Jan: 19 – 26 Aug: 9 – 18	Has a harbour and beaches, medium crime rate, excellent recreational facilities

1.2

Find the synonyms

Aim

To play a card game matching sentences which contain near synonyms

Language

Synonyms

Skills

Speaking

Lesson link

Use after Unit 1, SB p13

Materials

One copy of the worksheet cut up per group of four students. (Students will need access to a dictionary for the Extension activity)

Answers

(In the order cards appear on the worksheet)

talk/chat	chance/opportunity
thorough/carefully	alerts/warning
important/essential	grab/clasped
persuade/convince	wounded/injured
lie/deceive	trembled/shaking
gruesome/grisly	puzzling/perplexing

Extension:

extraordinary/unusual = remarkable. The words have the same meaning, although *extraordinary* is more emphatic. It can collocate with intensifying adverbs such as *absolutely* and *truly*, whereas *unusual* can't.

crouch = lower the body by bending the knees

stoop = lower the body by bending forward and down

excluded = prevented from entering somewhere or taking part in something

isolated = kept apart from someone else or other things

bundle = a collection of things fastened or wrapped together

parcel = something wrapped up for sending by post

Pre-activity (5 minutes)

- Call out words and ask students to tell you a synonym for each, e.g. *trust (faith), skilled (talented), persuade (convince), lie (deceive)*, etc.

Procedure (20 minutes)

- Explain that students are going to play a card game, matching sentences which contain near synonyms.

- Divide students into groups of four and give each group a set of cards, placed face down in a pile with the first card turned over so that it is face up on the table.

- Ask students to take it in turns to turn over a card from the pile. The student reads the sentence on the card to the rest of the group and checks that everybody understands what it means. If the playing student can match this card with a card which is already on the table, he/she keeps the pair. If not, he/she places the card face up on the table, and play passes to the next student. Go around checking and helping as necessary.

- The game continues until all the sentences have been matched. The student with the most pairs is the winner.

Extension (10 minutes)

- Ask students, in pairs, to write sentences to illustrate the following pairs of near synonyms: *extraordinary/unusual, crouch/stoop, excluded/isolated, bundle/parcel*. Go around helping with vocabulary as necessary.

- Have a class feedback session. Ask pairs to read their sentences to the class. Then discuss the differences in meaning between the synonyms (see Answers for definitions).

Sorry – I haven't got time to talk now.	Perhaps we can have a chat later on.
She gave the murder weapon a thorough examination.	Later she looked carefully around the room for clues.
An important part of the job is customer service.	It's essential to take good care of your clients.
There's no point trying to persuade him.	Why bother trying to convince him?
Don't lie to me about where you've been.	I'm sick of you trying to deceive me.
The horror film was very gruesome.	Some scenes were just too grisly to watch.
If I had the chance, I'd visit Australia.	It'd be a once in a lifetime opportunity.
The alarm alerts the police if anyone tries to break in.	It's a very effective warning system.
A thief tried to grab my bag.	When I clasped it to my side, he ran away.
The soldier was slightly wounded by the bomb.	Luckily no one else was injured.
The cashier's hands trembled as he handed over the money.	He was shaking with fear.
It was puzzling to find the door wide open.	It was even more perplexing to find that nobody was in.

1.3

Aim

To role play a radio debate about national stereotyping

Language

Expressing opinions

Agreeing and disagreeing

Managing a discussion

Skills

Reading, Listening, and Speaking

Lesson link

Use after Unit 1, SB p15

Materials

One copy of the worksheet cut up per group of three students

Pre-activity (5 minutes)

- Introduce the topic of national stereotypes with the class and discuss these questions: *Are national stereotypes generally humorous? In what situations might they not be humorous? How do students feel about how their nation is stereotyped?*

Procedure (30 minutes)

- Ask students if they know who *The Simpsons* are (a popular American cartoon about a family who live in a town called Springfield). Explain that students are going to read a newspaper article about an episode of *The Simpsons* which upset many of their Brazilian fans and then role play a radio show where a representative from the Brazil tourist board discusses the episode with a producer of the cartoon.

- Divide students into groups of three and give each group a copy of the newspaper article. Give students time to read the article and to check any items of vocabulary. Elicit students' reaction to the article and ask the following questions to check comprehension: *What image of Rio was 'The Simpsons' cartoon projecting? What do you think of the Rio tourist board's reaction? Was it an overreaction?*

- Give each student in the groups a different role card: A, B, or C. Give students time to read their role, look at the list of useful language, and prepare what they are going to say on the radio show. (You may like to pair Students A, Students B, and Students C during this preparation stage.) Go around helping with vocabulary as necessary.

- When everybody is ready, students role play the radio show with Student C managing the discussion. Go around listening, helping and correcting as necessary.

Extension (15 minutes)

- Ask students, in their groups of three, to write a letter to the producers of *The Simpsons*, either complaining about or supporting the episode. Remind students of letter conventions for formal letters, e.g. your address and date in the top right-hand corner, their address under and on the left of the page, *Dear Mr Smith* ending *Yours sincerely*, *Dear Sir/Madam* ending *Yours faithfully*, the use of formal language (i.e. no contractions or idiomatic expressions, etc.). Go around helping with vocabulary as necessary.

Blame it on *The Simpsons*

The Simpsons is one of the most popular comedy shows in the world, watched by millions of people every week. However, a recent episode set in Rio de Janeiro is proving less than funny for Brazilian fans. The show, which pokes fun at Latin American stereotypes, has enraged Rio's tourist board prompting them to sue Fox, the show's producers. They claim the show has undermined an $18 million advertising campaign to attract tourists to the city.

The episode called *Blame it on Lisa* is all about the family going to Rio in search of a poor orphan that Lisa (the daughter) has sponsored. It portrays Rio as a crime-ridden city where tourists are kidnapped by taxi drivers and mugged by gangs of children. The police are shown as lazy and unhelpful, violent monkeys prowl the streets and rats stop people crossing the road.

But the insults don't stop there. Many of the stereotypes picked on by the show are not Brazilian at all, but rather 'Latin American'. People speak with Spanish accents, men have moustaches and Brazilians are shown learning the macarena and dancing the conga (neither of which are performed in Brazil).

Playing on national stereotypes is nothing new for *The Simpsons*. In previous episodes English football hooligans, 'bland' Canadians, and 'uncultured' Australians have all been the butt of jokes.

Still, Rio's tourist secretary, José Eduardo Guinle, was not amused.

A

You are a producer of *The Simpsons*. You have been invited to a radio show to discuss the episode with a member of the Rio tourist board. You think the show was harmless and that people won't take it seriously. Note down arguments to support this point of view. Then prepare what you are going to say.

Here is some useful language to help you.

Expressing opinions
- In my opinion …
- As far as I'm concerned …
- The thing is …

Agreeing and disagreeing
- I couldn't agree more …
- I see your point but have you considered ….
- You have to see it from our point of view …
- No, really, I can't accept that …

Interrupting
- Yes, but what about the …?
- If I could just finish what I was saying …

B

You are a representative from the Rio tourist board. You have been invited to a radio show to discuss the episode with one of the producers from *The Simpsons*. You think the show was offensive and unfair and that people will take it seriously. Note down arguments to support this point of view. Then prepare what you are going to say.

Here is some useful language to help you.

Expressing opinions
- In my opinion …
- As far as I'm concerned …
- The thing is …

Agreeing and disagreeing
- I couldn't agree more …
- I see your point but have you considered …
- You have to see it from our point of view …
- No, really, I can't accept that …

Interrupting
- Yes, but what about the …?
- If I could just finish what I was saying …

C

You are a radio presenter. Your next show is about the media and national stereotypes. You have invited a member of the Rio tourist board and a producer from *The Simpsons* to discuss the recent episode set in Rio de Janeiro. Note down questions to ask your guests. Remember to manage the discussion and to make sure each person gets a chance to speak.

Here is some useful language to help you.

Managing a discussion
- Perhaps you could start by telling us …
- Could you say a bit more about …?
- I was interested in what you said about …
- What do you think about …?

Interrupting
- If I could just stop you there …
- To go back to what you were saying …
- So you think that …

1.4

Spot the word

Aim

To tell a story including American English words for other students to spot

Language

American and British English

Tense review

Skills

Speaking and Listening

Lesson link

Use after Unit 1, SB p16

Materials

One copy of the worksheet cut up per group of four students

Answers

Extension:

A holiday: holiday, petrol, trousers, twenty past eleven, a take-away

A dinner party: flat, dressing gown, cooker, vacuum cleaner, tap

A shopping trip: town centre, sales assistant, handbag, wardrobe, pavement

A job interview: lift, launderette, very, postman, spirits

A meal at a restaurant: bill, toilet, rubbish, main road, very tired

A crime: shop, pen knife, bank note, prison, district

A culture shock experience: queue, autumn, biscuit, car, far too strange

A sporting event: football, crisps, trainers, car park, postponement

A night at the cinema: Monday to Friday, badly lit, sweets, underground train, cinema

An accident: pram, doctor's surgery, plaster, traffic lights, chemist's

A long journey: ten to six, petrol station, lorries, timetable, newsagent

Moving house: post code, rent, post, removals van, transport café

Pre-activity (5 minutes)

- Explain to students that you are going to read out a story called 'A trip to the seaside' which has five American English words in it. Students should listen and note down the five words.
  *Last weekend, it was **awesome** weather, which is unusual for this time of year, so we decided to take advantage and go to the beach. We packed the **trunk** of the car with sandwiches, drinks, **candy**, and some deckchairs, and got to the beach at around ten **after** eleven. When we arrived, it was sunny but quite windy. It was too cold to go swimming, so we played **soccer** and then went for a walk along the sea front. All in all it was a lovely day out.*

- Check the answers with the class. Ask students to tell you the British English equivalents of the words (*great, boot, sweets, past, football*).

Procedure (25 minutes)

- Explain that students are going to tell a story for one minute including five American words for the others in their group to try and spot.

- Divide students into groups of four and give each group a set of cards in a pile, placed face down on the table. Explain that each card has the topic that students have to talk about and the five American words they have to include in their story.

- Ask each student in the groups to take a card. Tell students not to show each other their card. Give students time to check the words, if necessary, and to prepare their stories.

- Students take turns to talk for a minute including the five words in their story. The listening students, without conferring, write down any American English words they hear. You should act as time keeper calling out when to start and stop talking each time.

- The speaking student then tells the group the five words. Each listening student gets a point for each word he/she spotted.

- After everybody has talked for a minute, each student in the group takes another card and prepares to tell another story. When all the cards have been used, the student with the most points is the winner.

Extension (5 minutes)

- Ask students, in pairs, to note down the British English equivalents of the American English words on each card. Check the answers with the class.

vacation gas pants **A holiday** twenty after eleven a take-out	apartment bathrobe **A dinner party** range (n) vacuum faucet
downtown sales clerk **A shopping trip** purse closet sidewalk	elevator laundromat **A job interview** real (adv) mailman liquor
check (n) restroom **A meal at a restaurant** garbage freeway dead beat	store pocket knife bill **A crime** penitentiary precinct
stand in line fall (n) cookie **A culture shock experience** automobile way too strange	soccer chips sneakers **A sporting event** parking lot raincheck
Monday thru Friday badly lighted **A night at the cinema** candy subway train movie house	baby carriage doctor's office **An accident** band-aid stop signals drugstore
ten of six gas station **A long journey** trucks schedule news stand	zip code lease mail **Moving house** moving van truck stop

2.1

Aim

To complete a story with phrasal verbs which have more than one meaning, and to discuss the different meanings of the phrasal verbs

Language

Phrasal verbs with more than one meaning

Skills

Reading and Speaking

Lesson link

Use after Unit 2, SB p21

Materials

One copy of the worksheet cut in half per group of four students

Answers

1 A: turning down, B: turned down
2 A: give up, B: give up
3 A: takes to, B: takes to
4 A: get on (well) with, B: gets on with
5 A: turns up, B: turns up
6 A: put (Will) up, B: putting up
7 A: is going down with
   B: goes down (badly) with
8 A: work out, B: work out

The phrasal verbs in gaps 3, 4, 6, 7, and 8 have different meanings.

3 A: to start liking something/somebody B: to begin to do something as a habit
4 A: to have a friendly relationship with someone
   B: to do a job or task
6 A: to let someone stay in your house
   B: to display something
7 A: to start to become ill
   B: to describe how news is received
8 A: to find the answer
   B: to do physical exercise to keep fit

Pre-activity (5 minutes)

- Ask students to tell you how often they read novels. How do they decide what to read? Is it through a personal recommendation, reading a review, or reading a summary of the story on the back cover of the novel (the blurb)?

Procedure (25 minutes)

- Explain that students are going to read a gapped blurb of a novel and then complete the text with phrasal verbs.

- Divide students into an even number of pairs: A and B. (If you have an odd number of pairs, make two groups of three.) Give Pairs A worksheet A, and Pairs B worksheet B. Explain that Pairs A have a different blurb to Pairs B, but they will get the chance to read the other blurb later on. Give students time to read their blurbs and to check any items of vocabulary.

- Give students ten minutes to complete their blurbs with the correct form of the phrasal verbs. Go around helping as necessary. (Tell Pairs B not to worry about the out-of-sequence numbering in the gaps at this stage.)

- When students have finished, make groups of four with a Pair A and a Pair B. Explain that the same phrasal verbs were missing in each blurb and that the numbers for the gaps in each text correspond to the same phrasal verb (in the same or a different form). Give students, in their groups, a few minutes to check they used the same verb in each gap, and to read the other blurb.

- When groups have finished comparing their answers, ask them to look at how the phrasal verbs are used in each story and decide if they have the same meaning. If the meaning of the verb is different, students should discuss the difference in meaning. Go around helping as necessary.

- When everybody has finished, have a class feedback session.

Extension (20 minutes)

- Ask students to write a 100-word blurb for the last novel they read. Go around helping with vocabulary as necessary.

- Display the blurbs on the classroom wall. Give students time to read each other's blurbs and decide if they would like to read any of the novels based on the blurbs.

A

get on with

give up

go down with

put up

take to

~~turn down~~

turn up

work out

THE FLATMATE

Flats in London are always hard to find, and so are good flatmates.

After three weeks of (1) _turning down_ unsuitable tenants for her spare room, Kelly is ready to (2) _____ looking. Then Eileen answers her ad in the *Evening Post*. Eileen is friendly and open and Kelly immediately (3) _____ her. A week later she moves in. The two girls (4) _____ well _____ each other, until Eileen's brother, Will, unexpectedly (5) _____ . Eileen asks Kelly if she can (6) _____ Will _____ for a few weeks while he looks for a job. Although Kelly doesn't like Will, she feels she can't say no.

Will moves in and things start to go wrong. Eileen starts acting strangely and Kelly's cat disappears. Then Kelly begins to have violent headaches. She feels like she (7) _____ something, but she can't (8) _____ what it is. One day she gets home early and hears Eileen and Will arguing. It's only then that she realizes the awful truth ...

✂ -

B

get on with

give up

~~go down with~~

put up

take to

turn down

turn up

work out

Broken dreams

All Max ever wanted to be was an actor, so he quits college early and heads off to Hollywood. This (7) _goes down_ badly ___with___ his wealthy family, but Max is determined to succeed. Hollywood, however, is tougher than he imagined – he goes for audition after audition, but he's always (1) _____. Soon Max starts to run out of money, but he doesn't (2) _____ and go home. Instead he gets a job with a billboard company, (6) _____ posters on Sunset Boulevard.

Although he's far from happy with his new life, Max (4) _____ his new job, and continues to take acting classes and (8) _____ at a gym in the evening, but after a while he gets bored. He (3) _____ visiting a casino regularly and starts borrowing money from a local gangster called Red. After a night of heavy gambling, Max owes more money than he can pay. Two days later, Red (5) _____ at work. He wants his money, or Max's help with a robbery ...

2.2

Aim

To put a picture story in order, then tell the story

Language

Narrative tenses

Skills

Speaking

Lesson link

Use after Unit 2, SB p24

Materials

One copy of the worksheet cut up per pair of students

Useful vocabulary

nouns:
    desert island, survival skills, an SOS message, hut, shelter, storm, jungle

adjectives:
    remote, isolated, injured, shocked, desperate, exhausted, scorching

verbs:
    to crash, to be washed up, to set out (on a journey), to go well, to run out of (luck), to give up, to panic, to fight (for survival), to drown, to fall overboard

Answer

Correct order: f, b, j, e, i, a, h, c, g, d

Pre-activity (10 minutes)

- Ask students to think about a good book they have read recently. What was it that made the story interesting? Discuss ideas as a class (e.g. a strange or exciting situation, an interesting main character, unusual surroundings, an unexpected ending).

- Write *Shipwrecked* on board and check that everybody understands what it means. Explain that this is the title of the story students are going to tell. Brainstorm nouns, adjectives, and verbs that students might use in the story (see Useful vocabulary).

Procedure (30 minutes)

- Explain that students are going to put ten pictures in order to tell the story of a sailor called David Hanson who gets shipwrecked.

- Divide students into pairs and give each pair a jumbled set of picture cards. Give students time to discuss and predict the order of the story. (Tell students that labels a–j do not give the order.) Go around listening, asking students to explain why they have put the pictures in a particular order.

- When everybody has finished, explain that students are now going to tell the story. Ask them to consider the following points as they prepare (you might like to write them on the board):

  1 the main character (David Hanson): his age, appearance, and personality. What are his thoughts, feelings and reactions, his hopes and fears?

  2 the surroundings: the weather, the location. Is it calm/threatening/inhospitable?

  3 sequencing events: which linking words and time adverbials can you use (e.g. *by the time, after a while, suddenly,* etc.)?

  4 narrative tenses

- Give students time to practise telling the story. Encourage them to do so without referring to the pictures. Go round helping with vocabulary as necessary.

- When everybody is ready, tell students to swap partners. Explain that one student will start telling the story, without using the pictures, until you shout out 'swap', then their partner will carry on telling it. Students have to listen carefully to what their partner is saying so they know where they have got to in the story. Call out 'swap' several times during this phase.

Extension (15 minutes)

- Ask students, in pairs, to write up the story as a newspaper article. Remind them to use linking words and time adverbials to connect the events. Go around helping with vocabulary as necessary.

2.3

Sounds like ...

<table>
<tr><td>

Aim

To play a card game identifying words with the same pronunciation but different meanings (homophones)

Language

Homophones

Skills

Speaking

Lesson link

Use after Unit 2, SB p26

Materials

One copy of the worksheet cut up per pair of students

</td></tr>
</table>

Pre-activity (10 minutes)

- If necessary, remind students that in English there are words which have the same pronunciation but which are spelt differently and have different meanings, e.g. *through* and *threw*. These words are called homophones.
- Write the following words on the board and ask students to say and spell a homophone for each: *herd (heard), week (weak), tow (toe), some (sum)*.
- If your students are familiar with the phonetic symbols, ask them to write the homophones phonetically, e.g. /hɜːd/, /wiːk/, /təʊ/, /sʌm/.

Procedure (20 minutes)

- Explain that students are going to play Pelmanism where they match a word with the definition of its homophone, e.g. *break* with *the part of a vehicle that makes it go slower or stop* (brake).
- Divide students into pairs and give each pair a jumbled set of word cards and a jumbled set of definition cards, placed face down and spread out in two groups on the table.
- Students take it in turns to turn over one card from each group. If the word and the word which is defined are homophones, the student keeps the pair. If not, the cards are turned over and play passes to the other student. Go around helping as necessary. (The words which are defined are: *blue, serial, choose, pain, queue, weigh, pair, horse, flour, flu, guest, air*.)
- Students play until there are no more cards. The student with the most pairs wins.

Extension (10 minutes)

- Ask students, in their pairs, to write sentences to illustrate the meaning of the homophones on the word cards (i.e. the ones which weren't given as definitions). Go around helping with vocabulary as necessary.
- Have a class feedback session.

blew	cereal	chews
pane	cue	way
pear	hoarse	flower
flew	guessed	heir

A colour that when combined with yellow makes green	A single story in a magazine, on radio, or on television that is told in a number of parts over a period of time	To pick or select the person or thing that you prefer
The unpleasant feeling that you have when a part of your body has been hurt	A line of people, cars, etc. that are waiting for something or to do something	To measure how heavy something is, especially by using a machine
Two things that are almost the same and that are used together	A large animal that is used for riding on or for pulling or carrying heavy loads	A fine powder usually made from wheat and used for making bread, cakes, biscuits, etc.
An illness that is like a bad cold but more serious	A person that you invite to your home or your party	The mixture of gases that surrounds the earth and that people, animals, and plants breathe

3.1

Rainforest dilemma

Pre-activity (5 minutes)

- Ask students to tell you what they know about the problems facing the Amazon rainforests (e.g. destruction of the rainforest through mining and farming, loss of plant and wildlife, steady fall in the numbers of indigenous people, etc.).

Procedure (30 minutes)

- Explain that students either have an interest in or concerns about a proposed mining project in a remote part of the Amazon rainforest. They have been invited to go on a current affairs television programme called *News2night* to discuss their concerns/wishes and to try to reach an agreement on what should be done.

- Brainstorm some language students will need for expressing their point of view: *The reason I'm here is because …, I'd like to start by explaining / pointing out …, I believe that …, My reasons are as follows: first …, second …, As far as I'm concerned …,* etc. Then brainstorm some language students will need for negotiating and reaching an agreement, e.g. *We shouldn't do that unless …, That's a good idea providing that / on condition that / as long as …, What about …? We could consider …, That's out of the question, That seems reasonable,* etc.

- Divide students into groups of four and give each student a different role card. Give students time to read their role cards, check any items of vocabulary, and prepare to present their views at the meeting. Go around helping with vocabulary as necessary.

- When everybody is ready, ask groups to start the programme. Students take it in turns to introduce themselves and talk about their wishes/concerns. Then students discuss the issues and try to reach a compromise which will please all parties. Go around listening, helping and correcting as necessary. Make sure that everybody has a chance to speak.

- Have a class feedback session. Ask each group to tell the class about any decisions made and any agreements reached.

Extension (10 minutes)

- Write the following statement on the board: *Multinational companies are completely ruthless. They exploit Third-World economies for their own ends with little regard for environmental issues, human rights, or local industries.* Ask students, in small groups, to discuss the statement saying whether they agree or disagree with it, and if they can think of any examples which support or contradict this point of view. Go around listening and helping as necessary.

A

The local government is deciding on whether to grant mining licenses to companies to drill for gold, platinum, and diamonds in the rainforest. There is an estimated trillion dollars' worth of riches to be mined and over 700 mining licenses have been applied for.

You run a mine in the Amazon rainforest owned by a multinational company looking for gold, platinum, and diamonds. You support the mining licenses because, the way you see it, everyone wins. The government benefits because you are paying a huge mining license and taxes on the money you make. The local people benefit because they have jobs which enable them to support and feed their families. You don't see why you shouldn't take advantage of the country's natural resources. It's a good way to make money and progress, and means people's standard of living will steadily improve. It's a recipe for success, and that's how industrial nations develop.

B

The local government is deciding on whether to grant mining licenses to companies to drill for gold, platinum, and diamonds in the rainforest. There is an estimated trillion dollars' worth of riches to be mined and over 700 mining licenses have been applied for.

You are a miner. You want the mining licenses to be granted because you are dependent on mining for your living. Production in the mine where you work has dropped sharply and the mine is now almost exhausted. You will soon be out of work and you have a large family to support. Mining is the only way you can make money – there are no jobs for you in the city. You don't understand why people are making such a fuss about the licenses. The rainforest is huge, and you believe it should be used to help the people who live in it. You don't see why people like you should suffer for the environment.

C

The local government is deciding on whether to grant mining licenses to companies to drill for gold, platinum, and diamonds in the rainforest. There is an estimated trillion dollars' worth of riches to be mined and over 700 mining licenses have been applied for.

You are an environmentalist. You are alarmed by government plans to allow mining, and by the number of mining licenses applied for. If the mines are all built, the rainforest will shrink dramatically. The Amazon is big, but it takes years for the forest to regenerate itself. There would be a huge loss of animal species, and plant species with valuable medicinal qualities. The indigenous populations would also be badly affected. Over 50,000 km² of rainforest is destroyed a year and at that rate, the rainforest will disappear in 50 years' time. The implications for plant and animal life, for indigenous Indians, as well as the world's weather would be catastrophic.

D

The local government is deciding on whether to grant mining licenses to companies to drill for gold, platinum, and diamonds in the rainforest. There is an estimated trillion dollars' worth of riches to be mined and over 700 mining licenses have been applied for.

You represent the Yanomami and Kayapo Indians. Over the past decade your tribe has had to move deeper into the jungle as the rainforest slowly disappears. Now people are tired of moving, and are prepared to take radical action to protect themselves. Since farmers and miners started destroying the forest, many people in your tribe have been killed by diseases brought in by outsiders. The network of roads constructed to allow access to the mines will make it easier for people to reach this remote area. It will also be easier for diseases as well as fires to spread. There's a danger that the whole tribe could be destroyed.

3.2

Perfectly clear

Aim

To play a board game to practise adverb collocations

Language

Adverb collocations

Skills

Speaking

Lesson link

Use after Unit 3, SB p32

Materials

One copy of the worksheet per group of four students. Each group will need a coin and a watch with a second hand, and each student will need a counter

Suggested answers

carefully: 20, 21
deeply: 1, 5, 27
deliberately: 15, 16, 25
distinctly: 4, 28
eagerly: 13, 24
easily: 4, 15, 19, 25
exceptionally: 12, 18, 23
highly: 3, 10, 12, 27
hysterically: 7, 14, 25
perfectly: 4, 17, 19, 21, 23, 28
severely: 22, 27
utterly: 2, 11, 18
widely: 6, 8, 19, 27
wrongly: 9, 21, 26, 28

Pre-activity (5 minutes)

- Call out adjectives and verbs and ask students to tell you an adverb which collocates with each, e.g. *married (happily), wrong (totally), scared (easily), motivated (highly), love (passionately), affected (severely), thought through (carefully)*, etc.

Procedure (30 minutes)

- Explain that students are going to play a board game using adverbs and their collocates.
- Divide students into groups of four and give each group a copy of the board game.
- Students take it in turns to toss a coin to move around the board (heads = move one square, tails = move two squares). When they land on a square, students have fifteen seconds to choose an adverb from around the board which goes with the word on their square, and make a sentence. (In some cases, there are several adverbs which are appropriate.) If the playing student chooses an incorrect collocate, or cannot think of a sentence, he/she misses a turn. Go around listening and helping as necessary.
- The first student to get to the finish square wins the game.

Extension (10 minutes)

- Ask students, in pairs, to find four adverbs from around the board that can have more than one form. Ask students to write sentences illustrating the two forms of the adverbs.
- Have a class feedback session. Ask pairs to read their sentences to the class.

Extension:
1 easily/easy
   Susie passed her driving test easily.
   Go easy with the cream – I'm on a diet.
2 highly/high
   'Chicago' is a highly entertaining film.
   The kite was flying high overhead.
3 widely/wide
   It is widely known that global warming is getting worse.
   I didn't sleep very well last night. I was still wide awake at 3 a.m.
4 wrongly/wrong
   John was wrongly accused of shoplifting.
   When we arrived at the hotel, things started to go wrong.

severely

distinctly

finish

28 hear

27 affected

26 informed

deeply

highly

22 burnt

23 clear

24 rushed

25 upset

hysterically

21 worded

20 thought through

19 understood

18 stupid

utterly

wrongly

14 cried

15 scared

16 break

17 reasonable

eagerly

widely

13 awaited

12 talented

11 devastated

7 screamed

8 travelled

9 accused

10 amusing

carefully

easily

6 known

5 concerned

4 recall

3 motivated

deliberately

perfectly

exceptionally

start

1 regret

2 despise

3.3

Aim	
To present a new invention	
Language	
Presentation language	
Skills	
Reading, Writing, and Speaking	
Lesson link	
Use after Unit 3, SB p35	
Materials	
One copy of the worksheet per group of three students	

Answers

Paragraph 1:
I'm going to talk about / look at …
I'll begin by …
I'll start with …
Then I'm going to tell you …
Finally I'll look at / tell you …

Paragraph 2:
(It's) designed to …
(It) consists of …
This invention provides a …
This propels …
(It) has been developed to …
It's fitted with …
Tests have shown that …

Paragraph 3:
Our main market is …
They're also suitable for …
We intend to promote …
(It) will appeal to …

Pre-activity (5 minutes)

- Brainstorm new inventions from the past few years with the class (e.g. folding scooter, mobile phones with digital cameras, MP3 players, etc.).

Procedure (40 minutes)

- Explain that students are going to read the presentation notes for two inventions and then think of their own invention and present it to the class.

- Divide students into groups of three and give each group a copy of the worksheet. Give students time to read about the inventions and to check any items of vocabulary. Then ask them which invention they think is most/least useful and which they would be most/least likely to buy and why.

- Ask groups to look at the presentation notes again and tell you the purpose of each paragraph (paragraph 1: introduction; paragraph 2: what it's for, what it's made of, how it works; paragraph 3: who will buy it). Write this as a plan for a presentation on the board.

- Ask students to look at the kind of language used in each part of the presentations and to underline useful phrases (see Answers).

- Ask groups to think of their own invention. It could be something which helps them perform an everyday task more easily or to develop a specific skill. Suggest ideas if necessary (e.g. a bed which makes you get up in the morning, a car which is also a boat, a fold-away zebra crossing, an underwater bike, a napkin you can stick to your tie, etc.).

- Ask students to write a three-paragraph presentation for their invention. Tell them to refer to the models on the worksheet and use the paragraph plan on the board. Encourage students to draw a labelled diagram of their invention to use in their presentation. Go around helping with vocabulary as necessary.

- Tell groups that when they present their invention to the class, each student should read one paragraph. In their groups, students decide which paragraph they will read and how they will use their diagram in their presentation. Encourage students to memorize their paragraphs.

- When everybody is ready, groups take it in turns to present their invention. At the end of each presentation, encourage other groups to ask further questions about the invention, e.g. *I'd like to know a bit more about …, I didn't completely understand what you said about …,* etc.

Extension (5 minutes)

- Have a class vote for the most useful/interesting invention.

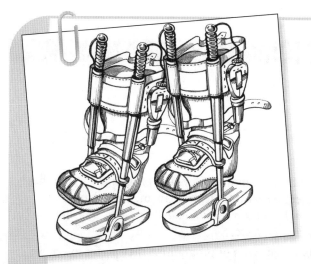

Petrol-powered boots

Today, I'm going to talk about an exciting new invention described as 'a giant leap for mankind'. I'll start with a description of what it is, then I'm going to tell you what it's made of and how it works. Finally, I'll look at who it's for, how people can use it, and how we intend to promote it.

The invention is a pair of petrol-powered boots designed to help you run at speeds of up to 40 kph – that's faster than the fastest Olympic sprinter! How can that be? Well, each boot consists of an engine and a tiny fuel tank. When the wearer steps down, the engine pushes a sprung metal platform away from the bottom of the boot. This propels the wearer up into the air. You can run for 25 minutes with the boots – or a distance of 16 kilometres!

So who will buy these boots? Well, just think about how you got here this morning. Were you stuck in a traffic jam? Was your train delayed? You've probably guessed by now that our main market is city commuters. Commuters can use the boots to avoid traffic jams and delays and get to work more quickly. They're also suitable for police officers, who can use the boots to chase criminals. In addition, we're currently developing a sports version for the teen market. We intend to promote the boots as the latest urban transport craze. In short, it's a faster alternative to the folding scooter.

Silent lawnmower

We're going to look at an original invention which will change life in suburbia for the better. I'll begin by describing what it is exactly, then we'll look at how it's constructed and how it works. Finally, I'll tell you who it's for and how it's going to change people's lives.

There's nothing more annoying than the sound of a lawnmower when you're trying to relax in your garden on a Sunday afternoon. Well, this invention provides a practical alternative – the bicycle lawnmower. This innovative machine has been developed to help people mow their lawns quickly and quietly. It's fitted with a car steering wheel for ease of use, and has two sets of bicycle gears so you can mow at different speeds. There's a mechanical mower at the front, and tests have shown that it's just as effective as an electric or petrol lawnmower.

Who will buy it? Well, we're sure that the invention will appeal to anyone with a garden. It's quieter than electric or petrol lawnmowers, and safer too, as there are no electric cables to cut, or petrol to spill. The main market for the lawnmower will probably be cities like Brussels, where on Sundays it's illegal to use a noisy lawnmower. But we're hoping its popularity will spread to everyone who likes gardening, as well as peace and quiet at the weekend.

4.1

The directors

<table>
<tr><td colspan="2">

Aim

To choose a new programme for a TV schedule

</td></tr>
</table>

Aim

To choose a new programme for a TV schedule

Language

Suggesting and recommending

Comparatives and superlatives

Skills

Reading, Listening, and Speaking

Lesson link

Use after Unit 4, SB p38, 39, & 40

Materials

One copy of the worksheet per student

Pre-activity (10 minutes)

- Brainstorm different types of television programmes with the class, and adjectives used to describe them, e.g. *a game show (lively, gripping), a sitcom (funny, addictive), a documentary (realistic, fascinating)*, etc.

- Ask students which types of programme they prefer to watch, how often they watch them, and when they usually watch them.

Procedure (30 minutes)

- Explain that students are directors of a television company. They are going to have a meeting to choose a programme for a Thursday evening slot to replace a sitcom which is coming to an end. Ask: *How do directors decide what programmes to show and when?* Brainstorm ideas with the class (e.g. their budget for the programme, the average age of the viewer at that time of day, what the competition channels are showing at the same time, how much money they can make from advertisers, etc.).

- Divide students into groups of four and give each student a copy of the worksheet. Give students time to read the memo with the notes on the possible replacement programmes available, and to check any items of vocabulary.

- Ask groups to talk about each programme in turn, discussing its good points and bad points in relation to the criteria they brainstormed earlier and the programme slot information on the worksheet, e.g. *I think 'Against the Clock' would be more appealing to the target age group than 'The Gift'. Although it's much more expensive, I think 'Life Swap' would guarantee us the best ratings,* etc. Go around listening, helping with vocabulary as necessary.

- When they have finished discussing each programme, ask groups to come to a decision about which programme to choose, e.g. *I think we should go with …, How about replacing the sitcom with …, I'm sure … is the most suitable,* etc.

- Have a class feedback session. Ask groups to tell the class which programme they chose and why.

Extension (10 minutes)

- In small groups, students tell each other about their favourite television programme. They should explain what type of programme it is, what happens in the programme, how often they watch it, and why they like it. Encourage students to use the adjectives they brainstormed in the pre-activity. Go around listening, helping as necessary.

MEMO

To: Directors

From: CEO

Re: Replacement programme for 'Our House'

As you aware, 'Our House', the company's most popular sitcom to date, is coming to an end in the next few weeks and we have to decide on a new programme to replace it. Below is a list of possibilities. Please read the notes and the programme slot information in preparation for the board meeting on Wednesday at 2 p.m.

Programme slot information

- The programme slot is 8 p.m. to 9 p.m. on a Thursday night.
- It is after the news and before the Thursday movie.
- The original sitcom was popular with teenagers and viewers in their early twenties.
- If possible, we want to keep the same audience and the same advertisers.
- We have a limited budget for the show.
- A rival channel is airing a popular and established celebrity game show at the same time.

View from the top — price: €€€

A gritty documentary which follows and interviews different politicians each week. Experience some of the day-to-day problems facing leading politicians, then step back and look at the big picture as our lively studio audience questions this week's guest.

Against the Clock — price: €

A fast-paced show where contestants quickly learn that time costs money. Watch as contestants battle against the clock to answer as many questions as they can. Will they finish before the buzzer, or will they come up against a wild card question? Both educational and fun, you never know who's going to win in 'Against the Clock'.

Life Swap — price: €€

'Life Swap' is a fly-on-the-wall documentary that takes a look at how twenty-something singles run their lives. Every week different contestants have the chance to experience someone else's routine: how they run their home, how they cope with work pressures, what they spend their money on, and what they do in their free time. At the end of the week, contestants get together and tell each other what they think of their new life. 'Life Swap' is a fascinating opportunity to witness what it's like to be 'in someone else's shoes'.

The Gift — price: €€€€

A cult teen series about a girl with special powers. Blueberry High looks like any other High School and Amy Harris looks like any other senior. But things are not quite what they seem. In this gripping twelve-part series, viewers learn the sinister truth about Blueberry's shady past, and find out about Amy's unusual gift.

Celebrity Chat — price: €€€€

So you thought you knew everything about your favourite pop idol or movie star? 'Celebrity Chat' hosted by Zara (a well-known celebrity herself) delves deeper than *Hello!* magazine and the tabloid newspapers. Tactful and thoughtful, Zara encourages celebrities to reveal surprising facts about themselves and their families. Confessional TV at its best.

Can you believe it? — price: €€

Each week 'Can you believe it?' introduces more thrilling stunts from the world of Hollywood film makers. From hair-raising car crashes to breath-taking bungee jumps, you'll barely believe your eyes in 'Can you believe it?'

Talking Movies — price: €

What's the latest gossip about Leonardo DiCaprio? Is Nicole Kidman working with Steven Spielberg? Direct from LA, 'Talking Movies' looks at intriguing 'insider' stories on what's happening in Tinsel Town. There's also a round-up of this week's movies and the box office top ten.

4.2

Aim
To play a card game using discourse markers

Language
Discourse markers, e.g. *as I was saying, actually, apparently*

Skills
Speaking

Lesson link
Use after Unit 4, SB p42

Materials
One copy of the worksheet cut up per group of four students. Each group will need a watch with a second hand

Pre-activity (10 minutes)

- Write the following phrases on the board: *quite honestly, all in all, though, mind you, as I was saying, as a matter of fact.* Ask students what the phrases are used for, e.g. *quite honestly* (to give an opinion), *all in all though* (to sum up), *mind you* (to introduce a different point of view or another idea), *as I was saying* (to go back to a previous point), *as a matter of fact* (to reinforce a point you have already made).

- Brainstorm other discourse markers with the class. Ask students if any of the discourse markers fit into the categories above, e.g. *to tell you the truth* (to give an opinion), *at the end of the day* (to sum up), *that said* (to introduce a different point of view or another idea), *what I wanted to say was* (to go back to a previous point), etc.

Procedure (30 minutes)

- Explain that students are going to play a game where they talk for 30 seconds about a topic and include a discourse marker. Write *celebrities* and *quite honestly* on the board and invite a confident student to talk about celebrities for 30 seconds, and to try and include the discourse marker, e.g. *I think celebrities have a hard time because they have absolutely no private life. Quite honestly, I wouldn't want to be famous,* etc.

- Divide students into groups of four and give each group a set of topic cards and a set of discourse marker cards, placed face down on the table in two piles. Ask each group to nominate a time-keeper.

- Students take it in turns to pick up a card from each pile. They talk for 30 seconds about the topic and try to include the discourse marker that they have picked up. If they speak without pausing or repeating themselves for 30 seconds, they keep the topic card. If they use the discourse marker naturally and correctly, they also get to keep that card. Go around listening, noting down any common errors to go over at the end.

- Students play until there are no more cards. The student with the most cards wins.

Extension (15 minutes)

- Choose one of the topics from the worksheet, e.g. *reality shows,* and ask students, in small groups, to discuss the topic using discourse markers when they are giving their opinions. Go around listening, helping as necessary.

- Have a class feedback session. Ask groups to report back to the class what they said about the topic. Ask the class if they agree or disagree with these opinions and why.

designer clothes	Hollywood films	piracy – CDs, DVDs	government health warnings
education	journalists	plastic surgery	Third-World aid
extreme sports	marriage	reality shows	TV advertisements
genetic engineering	mobile phones	space travel	UFOs
global warming	nuclear power	the Internet	your country's leader
actually	as a matter of fact	mind you	quite honestly
admittedly	as I was saying	naturally	so to speak
all in all, though	at least	no doubt	still
anyway	clearly	obviously	surprisingly
apparently	I mean	of course	to tell you the truth

4.3

Aim
To play dominoes, matching question tags to statements

Language
Question tags
Intonation

Skills
Speaking

Lesson link
Use after Unit 4, SB p46

Materials
One copy of the worksheet cut up per group of three to four students

Pre-activity (5 minutes)

- Call out some statements and ask students to tell you the question tag for each, checking that they use the correct intonation each time, e.g. *He speaks Russian, (doesn't he?), You didn't tell him about the other night, (did you?), So, you've been to Paris, (have you?), Close the door, (will you?),* etc. Point out that the intonation in question tags can rise or fall depending on whether the person is asking for confirmation or asking a genuine question, e.g.

  A *You don't like Emma, do you?* (rising)
  B *Yes, I do. She's really nice. What made you say that?*

  or

  A *You don't like Emma, do you?* (falling)
  B *No, not really. We haven't got much in common.*

Procedure (15 minutes)

- Explain that students are going to play dominoes with question tags.

- Divide students into groups of three to four and give each group a set of dominoes, placed face down in a pile on the table.

- Ask one student in each group to shuffle the dominoes and to deal them equally to each person in the group.

- Another student starts by placing a domino on the table. Then students take it in turns to put one domino next to a matching statement or tag. If a student can't play, he/she misses a turn. Go around listening, helping and correcting as necessary.

- The student who gets rid of all his/her dominoes first wins the game.

- Have a class feedback session. Ask students to read out the questions on the dominoes using the correct intonation each time depending on whether they are asking for confirmation or asking a genuine question.

Extension (10 minutes)

- Ask students, in pairs, to write statements which match the following tags:

  ..., will you?   ..., shall we?   ..., doesn't he?   ..., isn't it?
  ..., can't they?   ..., do you?   ..., won't we?   ..., aren't I?

  Tell them to be as imaginative as they can. Go around helping and correcting as necessary.

- When students have finished, ask pairs to swap their sentences with another pair. Pairs take it in turns to read out the sentences using the correct intonation.

can he?	So you've seen the film,	have you?	Pass me the remote control,
will you?	Let's hit the road,	shall we?	They come from Mars,
don't they?	You're just bone idle,	aren't you?	You haven't paid the bill,
have you?	So it works now,	does it?	He's already given in,
has he?	She's running late,	isn't she?	He hasn't turned up yet,
has he?	They know how to party,	don't they?	She's very understanding,
isn't she?	You're working with Max,	aren't you?	Give me a hand,
will you?	Tell me the truth,	won't you?	He eats like a horse,
doesn't he?	It doesn't look promising,	does it?	Let's get a takeaway,
shall we?	The weather was looking bad,	wasn't it?	It was really an accident,
wasn't it?	You won't take no for an answer,	will you?	He can't have been selected,
can he?	You'll be taking the car,	won't you?	He can't have finished so soon,

5.1

Aim
To role play an interview with a person who won his/her spouse in a radio competition

Language
Indirect and negative questions
Fluency practice

Skills
Reading, Listening, and Speaking

Lesson link
Use after Unit 5, SB p48, 49, & 50

Materials
One copy of the worksheet cut up per pair of students

Pre-activity (10 minutes)

- Read out the following statements one by one and ask students if they agree or disagree with them and why:
  1 *Marriage brings stability to a relationship.*
  2 *Arranged marriages are a good idea.*
  3 *You should only marry your soul mate.*
  4 *Women should propose to men.*
  5 *Marriage should be for life.*

Procedure (30 minutes)

- Explain that students are going to read a newspaper article about an unusual wedding and then interview either the husband or wife from the article. Write the following newspaper headline on the board: *The lottery of love.* Ask students to predict what the newspaper story is about.

- Divide students into pairs and give each pair a copy of the newspaper article. Give students time to read the article, check their predictions, and any items of vocabulary. Ask: *Were you fascinated, horrified, or amused by the story? What image of marriage does it project? Do you think the marriage will last? Why / Why not?*

- Explain that in each pair, Student A is either the man or woman from the newspaper article, and Student B is the journalist who is going to interview him/her for a magazine article. Give Students A worksheet A, and Students B worksheet B. Give students time to read their role cards and prepare what they are going to say. (You may like to pair Students A and Students B during this preparation stage.) Go around helping with vocabulary.

- Remind Students B to be polite and use indirect questions. If necessary, brainstorm a list of indirect question prompts, e.g. *Could you tell me …? Would you mind telling me …? I wonder if you …?* etc. Students B should also ask negative questions to express surprise, e.g. *But didn't your parents try to stop you going on the show?*

- When everybody is ready, students act out the interview. Go round listening, helping and correcting as necessary.

- Invite one or two pairs to act out their interview at the front of the class.

Extension (10 minutes)

- Ask students, in pairs, to make a list of ten ingredients for a successful marriage.

- Have a class feedback session. Can the class agree on ten?

The lottery of love

In May, almost every newspaper had photos of Ian Grey and Holly Anderton on their front page. The couple weren't film stars, they hadn't broken a record, and they hadn't committed a crime – in fact they hardly knew each other. Ian and Holly were the winners of a competition held by a Manchester radio station. Their prize was each other.

The wedding was announced after votes were cast by radio listeners who had been following the show for weeks. The 'happy' couple were understandably 'delighted' because as well as winning a £50,000 wedding, they also won a honeymoon in the Bahamas and a smart flat in Manchester. Many people were horrified by the show, branding it as the ultimate insult to marriage and a cheap publicity stunt. However other people were fascinated: could this 'arranged' lottery of love actually work?

A

You have just 'won' a husband/wife on a radio game show. You're very excited about it, and have arranged an interview with a journalist to talk about your wedding. Make notes about your experience to date, e.g. why you entered the show, what you think about your new spouse, how your family and friends have reacted, who you have invited to the wedding, what you think is the recipe for a successful marriage, if you seriously think the marriage will last, etc.

B

You are a journalist and have been asked to interview a man/woman who has just 'won' a wife/husband on a radio game show. You want to find out as much as possible about the man/woman, in particular why they decided to do it. Note down seven questions your readers would want answered, e.g. why they entered the show, what they thought when they first saw their new husband/wife, things they know about their husband/wife, how their family and friends have reacted, who is going to the wedding, what they think is the recipe for a successful marriage, if they think the marriage will last, etc.

5.2

The wedding planner

Suggested answer

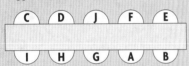

Clara can sit opposite Ivan and talk to him about art and opera and next to her husband.

David can sit next to Julia and talk about home improvements. He probably won't have anything to say to Helen, but he doesn't have children, so they probably won't argue.

Julia can sit in between David and Frank. Frank will be patient with her if she's rude and will probably listen to her problems if she wants to talk about them. She will sit opposite Greg who is easy to get on with.

Frank will sit in between Julia and Ella, who will probably want to talk about her wedding. He will sit opposite Anna, who is quite shy. Ella sits next to Frank and opposite Ben and Anna who are expecting a baby. Ella can talk about starting a family, and avoid mentioning work.

Greg can sit next to Anna so they can talk about Africa. Helen sits next to Ivan. They can talk about art and music.

Pre-activity (5 minutes)

- Ask students if they have ever been to a dinner party where the table seating was pre-arranged. Ask: *Did you have things in common with the people sitting next to you? Was it a good evening?*

- Brainstorm criteria that people might use when arranging a seating plan for a formal party (e.g. peoples' personalities, their interests, if they are part of a couple, etc.).

Procedure (30 minutes)

- Explain that students are wedding planners and they have been left a task by their boss to organize the seating plan for a table at a wedding reception.

- Divide students into pairs and give each pair a copy of the worksheet. Give students time to read the note from the boss and the information about the ten people to be seated at the table.

- Ask pairs to discuss the people, e.g. *The thing about Clara is she's quite loud and opinionated, but I think she and Ivan might be able to talk about opera*, etc. and then agree on the best seating plan. Go around listening, helping as necessary.

- When everybody has finished, have a class feedback session. Ask students to tell the class their seating plan and to explain why they arranged it in this way.

Extension (10 minutes)

- Ask students, in pairs, to imagine and write down the conversation between two of the people sitting next to each other in their seating plan. Students can take it in turns to act out their conversation in front of the class.

The Wedding Planner

Help! I can't work out the table arrangement for these people for Susan and Richard's wedding reception. I've had a long conversation with Susan on the phone and she's given me the following information – she's also keen that we have an arrangement of male, female, male, etc. I need the table arrangement by three o'clock this afternoon. Can you fax it to me at home? Thanks. Jenny.

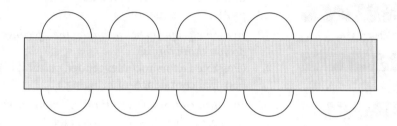

Anna is married to Ben and works for an Aid organization. She likes to discuss Third-World problems and is also interested in animal rights. She's expecting a baby. She's quite shy.

Ben is a computer programmer. He's happily married to Anna. He's quite sociable, but he doesn't like talking about work.

Clara is a housewife, married to David. She's very well off and spends most of her husband's money on jewellery and fur coats. She's quite loud and opinionated. She loves going to the opera.

David has his own building firm. He's sociable and confident. He loves talking about money and work.

Ella has just got engaged to Frank. She's a journalist so she doesn't earn much money. At the moment, all she can think about is her own wedding and starting a family.

Frank is a vet and has just got engaged to Ella. He's very patient and a good listener.

Greg is single and works for a travel agent. He does a lot of independent travelling and is keen to talk about his recent trip to Africa. He's very easy to get on with.

Helen is a single mother, bringing up a small child. She teaches music at a school for children with learning disabilities. She has quite strong opinions about child care.

Ivan is an artist and unhappily married to Julia. He's quite sensitive and extremely cultured. He often goes to the opera and visits art galleries.

Julia is unhappily married to Ivan. They often argue when they go out together. She can be quite rude at times. Her interests are art, shopping, and home improvements.

5.3

Aim
To discuss gender stereotypes, and then to continue a story
Language
Narrative tenses
Skills
Reading, Speaking, and Writing
Lesson link
Use after Unit 5, SB p54
Materials
One copy of the worksheet cut in half per two students

Pre-activity (10 minutes)

- Write the following questions on the board and explain any new vocabulary:

  1 *Is it always a good thing to show your emotions? In which situations might it be better to 'bottle things up'?*
  (Possible answers: It's more honest to show your feelings; it's unhealthy not to. It's not a good idea to show emotions in professional situations.)

  2 *Are some people better at hiding their feelings than others? Why do you think this is?*
  (Possible factors include: gender, cultural background, personal confidence, upbringing.)

  3 *In which cultures do you think it's more acceptable to show your feelings? In which is it less acceptable?*

- Give students, in pairs, a few minutes to discuss the questions. Then have a class feedback session.

Procedure (35 minutes)

- Explain that students are going to read an extract from a story, where the details about the characters (age, gender, name, etc.) have been omitted.

- Divide students into groups of two to four and give each student a copy of the worksheet. (The text is reproduced twice on the worksheet for ease of copying.) Give students time to read the extract and to check any items of vocabulary.

- Ask students, in their groups, to discuss the questions about the extract. Go around listening, helping as necessary. When everybody has finished, have a class feedback session.

- Ask students, in their groups, to write the next paragraph of the story. Go around helping with vocabulary as necessary.

- When everybody is ready, ask groups to read out their paragraph to the class and then vote on the best one.

Extension (10 minutes)

- Write the following statement on the board: *Women are more in touch with their emotions than men.* Ask students, in their groups, to discuss whether they agree or disagree with the statement and to think of reasons to support their opinion.

- Have a class feedback session.

A BRIEF ENCOUNTER

It was a perfect morning for a walk. A metallic-blue sea crashed over the rocks below, and a fresh wind rushed past as I made my way along the rugged coastline. It was early and there weren't many people about, but as I was walking along the cliff top I noticed a solitary figure huddled on a weathered bench looking out to sea. It looked like a _____ . _____ had a small rucksack over one shoulder and _____ seemed to be clutching a letter in _____ hand. There was something about _____ that made me feel uneasy. As I got closer _____ looked up and stared – a blank stare from a striking, tear-stained face. I put on a friendly smile and asked _____ , 'Everything all right?' _____ nodded and immediately looked away. I hesitated, 'Are you sure?' 'I'm fine, really,' _____ said in a determined way, at the same time blushing and fighting back the tears. I hesitated briefly, then carried on with my walk, but I couldn't help wondering – and worrying – about the _____ . On the spur of the moment I decided to go back …

1 **Read the text about a chance meeting and answer the following questions.**

   a Where does the story take place?

   b Do you think the narrator is male or female? How old do you think the narrator is? How would you describe the narrator: protective, thoughtful, condescending, interfering, weary, impetuous, responsible?

   c Who do you think the 'solitary figure' is? Is it a man or a woman, a boy or a girl?

   d What was unusual about the two people? Why do you think each of them was there?

   e If you were the narrator, what would you have done?

2 **Write the next paragraph of the story. Consider the following questions.**

   a Was the person still there?

   b What did the narrator do/say?

   c What happened in the end?

✂ -

A BRIEF ENCOUNTER

It was a perfect morning for a walk. A metallic-blue sea crashed over the rocks below, and a fresh wind rushed past as I made my way along the rugged coastline. It was early and there weren't many people about, but as I was walking along the cliff top I noticed a solitary figure huddled on a weathered bench looking out to sea. It looked like a _____ . _____ had a small rucksack over one shoulder and _____ seemed to be clutching a letter in _____ hand. There was something about _____ that made me feel uneasy. As I got closer _____ looked up and stared – a blank stare from a striking, tear-stained face. I put on a friendly smile and asked _____ , 'Everything all right?' _____ nodded and immediately looked away. I hesitated, 'Are you sure?' 'I'm fine, really,' _____ said in a determined way, at the same time blushing and fighting back the tears. I hesitated briefly, then carried on with my walk, but I couldn't help wondering – and worrying – about the _____ . On the spur of the moment I decided to go back …

1 **Read the text about a chance meeting and answer the following questions.**

   a Where does the story take place?

   b Do you think the narrator is male or female? How old do you think the narrator is? How would you describe the narrator: protective, thoughtful, condescending, interfering, weary, impetuous, responsible?

   c Who do you think the 'solitary figure' is? Is it a man or a woman, a boy or a girl?

   d What was unusual about the two people? Why do you think each of them was there?

   e If you were the narrator, what would you have done?

2 **Write the next paragraph of the story. Consider the following questions.**

   a Was the person still there?

   b What did the narrator do/say?

   c What happened in the end?

6.1

April fool

Answers

Extension:

A

A convict caught the wrong bus when he was trying to escape from prison.

Movie posters have been developed which can talk back to people.

Someone's attempt at smuggling a python into the country has failed.

A stunt plane was landed by accident on a passing car.

B

A prisoner escaped from one prison and broke into another.

Some celebrities are going to have holidays in outer space.

A couple out on a blind date discovered a strange/funny coincidence.

The world's first ironing robot has been revealed by scientists.

Pre-activity (10 minutes)

- Ask students which special days their country celebrates each year. Ask if anyone celebrates *April 1st*. Explain that it is a special day in the UK and find out if anybody knows why. (April 1st is called 'April fool's day' and is traditionally a day when people play light-hearted tricks on each other. It originated in 1562 when New Year was moved from April 1st to January 1st.)

- Ask students what type of tricks people might play on April 1st. Explain that in the UK many newspapers publish strange, but true stories, as well as false or 'trick' stories on this day. Ask students if they have ever read a false story or had a trick played on them on April fool's day.

Procedure (45 minutes)

- Explain that students are journalists and that they have two strange, but true stories for the April 1st edition of their newspaper. Students are going to write a third story which is equally strange, but which isn't true.

- Divide students into two groups: A and B. Divide students in each group into smaller groups of two or three. There should be an equal number of groups in A and B. Give students in Group A worksheet A, and students in Group B worksheet B.

- Give groups time to read their two stories, check any items of vocabulary, and read the instructions for their own story.

- In their groups, students write their own story. Go around helping with vocabulary as necessary and encouraging students to use passive constructions where appropriate.

- When groups have completed their story, ask students to choose one story each and practise telling it from memory.

- When students have finished, combine a Group A with a Group B. Students in Group A take it in turns to tell one of the stories from memory. When the three stories have been told, students in Group B try to identify the false story. When they have finished, Group B presents its stories, and students in Group A try to identify the false story. Go around listening.

- Have a class feedback session. Ask students which of their stories they thought was the least believable, the funniest, or the most predictable, and to say why.

Extension (5 minutes)

- Ask students, in their original groups, to rewrite the four newspaper headlines at the bottom of their worksheet as complete sentences. Remind them to add articles, pronouns, etc. and to decide on which tenses to use.

- Check the answers with the class.

A

Man stuck in chimney was chasing his parrot

A man who spent almost seventeen hours stuck inside the chimney of a shop in Indiana told police he was following his parrot. The man said he was walking his parrot when it managed to escape, fly onto the roof, and go down the chimney. Apparently he got stuck trying to follow it. The man was rescued by fire-fighters who were alerted after the shop's owner heard him calling for help.

It's not known whether he'll be arrested and charged with burglary.

Man fires pumpkin

A cannon has been invented in the US which can fire a pumpkin more than 1,000 metres. The invention has an eight-metre barrel and is powered by a 2,000-litre air tank. It's named 'Ain't all there' and is said to be capable of propelling the average pumpkin at 1,200 kph.

Jim Bristoe, a 42-year-old electrician and mechanic, recently test-fired the pumpkin. Unfortunately, it went off course, and shattered the rear window of a car parked nearby. Fortunately, no casualties were reported.

Your story

Your story should be about 100 words. Decide on the content: will it be a crime that went wrong, a funny accident, a strange coincidence, a weird invention, a bizarre competition, or an amazing discovery? Make your story as amusing or imaginative as possible, but take care that the details sound true. Invent facts, names of people, places, and organizations, etc. to add credibility to your story.

You can choose a headline from the list below or invent your own story.

- Escaped convict catches wrong bus
- Movie posters talk back
- Smuggled python attempt fails
- Stunt plane lands on passing car

B

Dog ads innovation

A London-based advertising company says it plans to recruit a number of dogs to carry adverts called 'dogverts'. The idea has already been tested on golden Labrador, Fido, who carried an ad for a PlayStation II game. To qualify as dogverts, dogs need to be healthy, have short, pale hair (so the advertisements can be seen), and must be walked regularly.

If the tests are successful, the campaign is expected to spread throughout the country. Richard Williams, senior marketing manager of the company said, 'Only vegetable dyes are used, so the dogs aren't harmed in any way.'

Teenager lived on chewing gum in jungle ordeal

A British teenager who was lost for three days in the Australian rainforest says she survived her ordeal by eating chewing gum. Louise Saunders found her own way out of the dense bushland in northern Queensland while attempts by the police to locate her were under way. The nineteen-year-old had been missing since Tuesday morning when she set out alone on a hike. During the first hour of her walk she ate a banana, but the rest of the time she survived on sugar-free gum. 'I'll always thank chewing gum for my survival,' she said.

Your story

Your story should be about 100 words. Decide on the content: will it be a crime that went wrong, a funny accident, a strange coincidence, a weird invention, a bizarre competition, or an amazing discovery? Make your story as amusing or imaginative as possible, but take care that the details sound true. Invent facts, names of people, places, and organizations, etc. to add credibility to your story.

You can choose a headline from the list below or invent your own story.

- Prisoner breaks into prison
- Celebs to holiday in outer space
- Blind date coincidence
- World's first ironing robot revealed

6.2

Aim

To complete a crossword by asking for and giving definitions for nouns formed from phrasal verbs

Language

Nouns formed from phrasal verbs

Skills

Speaking and Listening

Lesson link

Use after Unit 6, SB p60

Materials

One copy of the worksheet cut in half per pair of students

Pre-activity (5 minutes)

- Define the following words for students to guess: *bought at a restaurant for eating somewhere else (takeaway), sudden start of a war or appearance of an illness (outbreak), something which prevents the progress of something (setback), a delay or an armed robbery (hold-up).*

Procedure (25 minutes)

- Explain that students are going to work in pairs to complete a crossword puzzle with nouns formed from phrasal verbs. Students are going to take it in turns to give definitions to their partner.
- Divide students into pairs. Give Students A worksheet A, and Students B worksheet B. Tell students not to show each other their worksheets.
- Give students time to write definitions or to write gapped sentences which illustrate the meaning of the words on their puzzle. Encourage students to make their sentences and definitions as clear as possible, but tell them to avoid using the verb form of the word, e.g. they cannot define the word *cutback* as *when you cut back on something.* Go round helping with vocabulary as necessary. (You may like to pair Students A and Students B during this preparation stage.)
- Students work in pairs to complete the crossword by asking and answering, e.g. *What's 1 down? What's 2 across?* etc. Go round listening, helping and correcting as necessary.
- Students can compare their crosswords at the end to check they have completed them correctly.

Extension (5 minutes)

- Ask students which of the compound nouns in the crossword cannot operate as phrasal verbs (*backlash, showdown*).

A

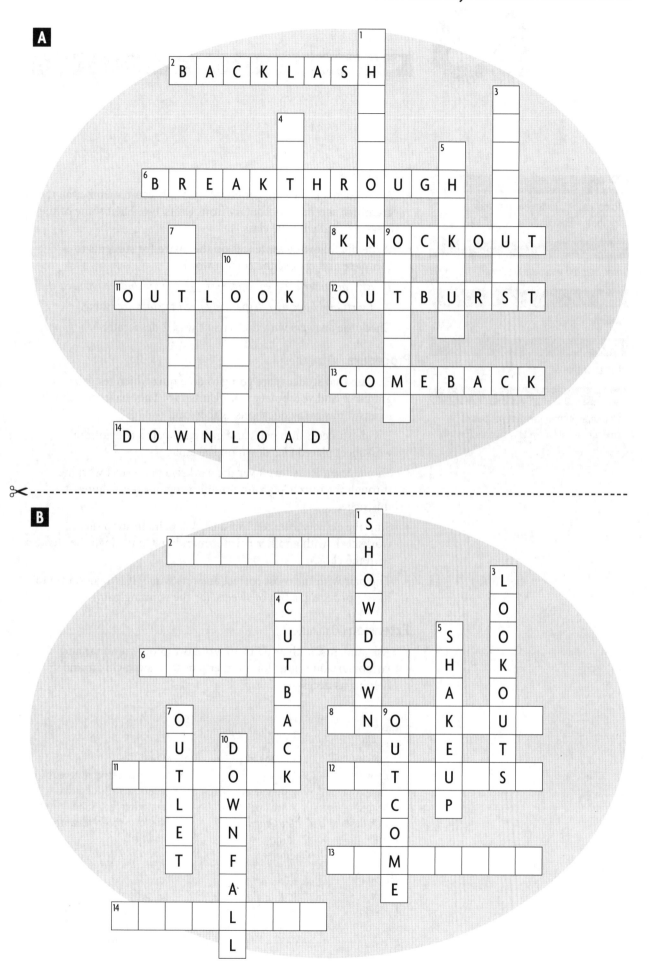

B

6.3

Race against time! 1

Aim

To do a quiz to revise grammar and vocabulary from Units 1–6

Language

Grammar and vocabulary review

Skills

Reading

Lesson link

Use after Unit 6

Materials

One copy of the worksheet per pair of students. A bag of sweets or similar for a prize

Pre-activity (5 minutes)

- Ask students if they are confident that they can remember all the grammar and new vocabulary from Units 1–6. Elicit some of the areas covered with the class.
- Write the following sentences on the board for students to complete and choose the correct word:

  1 *My computer isn't working. If it _____ , you could have used it.*

  2 *I virtually / deeply / desperately need to start exercising.*

- Check the answers with the class (1 was, 2 desperately).

Procedure (30 minutes)

- Explain that students are going to do a quiz which tests the grammar and vocabulary from Units 1–6. They have ten minutes to answer as many questions as they can.
- Divide students into pairs and give each pair a copy of the worksheet placed face down on the table.
- Shout: *Start!* Pairs turn over the worksheet and start working through the quiz. Go around monitoring but not helping at this stage.
- Stop the activity after ten minutes. Ask pairs to swap their worksheets with another pair for marking. Go through the answers with the class.
- The pair with the most correct answers wins. (It is a good idea to have a prize, e.g. a bag of sweets, for the winning pair.)

Extension (10 minutes)

- Ask students, in their pairs, to write two more grammar and vocabulary questions for another pair to answer. Go around helping as necessary.

Answers
Grammar

1 hadn't	8 wouldn't they	14 to be
2 couldn't	9 He's hurt	15 A strike has been threatened by
3 do	10 is being questioned	trade unions. / Trade unions
4 neither	11 A film that I love is	have threatened a strike.
5 have they	*The Godfather*.	16 Plans for a robbery have been
6 with	12 losing	uncovered.
7 just	13 expected	

Vocabulary

1 yard	5 strategy	9 shyly	13 perfectly
2 check	6 talented	10 cry	14 deeply
3 Dutch	7 random	11 contempt	15 love and war
4 Peruvian	8 striking	12 tension	16 never did run smooth

RACE AGAINST TIME!

Grammar

Complete the sentences.

1 I thought I'd seen the film, but I _____ .

2 He wanted to finish the marathon, but he _____ . It was just too difficult.

3 I might go away this summer. If I _____ , I'll visit France.

4 He doesn't smoke, and _____ do I.

5 They haven't set off yet, _____?

6 I feel dreadful. I think I'm going down _____ a cold.

7 I've _____ read an amazing book!

8 They'd have remembered to lock the door, _____?

Correct the mistakes.

9 'What's up with Ben?' 'He's been hurting his leg skiing.'

10 The suspect is questioning by the police this afternoon.

11 A film is *The Godfather* that I love.

12 What she'll never get over is lose the race.

13 It is expect that Detective Green will solve the crime.

14 He is assumed be working for the government.

Write the newspaper headlines in full.

15 Strike threat by trade unions

_____

16 Robbery plans uncovered

_____

Vocabulary

Complete the sentences.

1 The American word for *garden* is _____ .

2 The American word for *bill* is _____ .

3 Someone from the Netherlands is _____ .

4 A _____ is someone from Peru.

5 A synonym for *tactics* is _____ .

6 A synonym for *skilled* is _____ .

7 A synonym for *haphazard* is _____ .

8 A synonym for *stunning* is _____ .

9 A synonym for *bashfully* is _____ .

10 An antonym for *laugh* is _____ .

11 An antonym for *admiration* is _____ .

12 An antonym for *relaxation* is _____ .

Choose the correct alternative.

13 It's *distinctly / perfectly / virtually* clear that he can't speak Spanish.

14 She was *highly / deeply / eagerly* worried about the exam.

Complete the proverbs.

15 All's fair in _____ .

16 The course of true love _____ _____ .

7.1

Graffiti wisdom

Aim
To match halves of graffiti quotations

Language
Fluency practice

Skills
Speaking

Lesson link
Use after Unit 7, SB p63

Materials
One copy of the worksheet cut up per group of ten students

Pre-activity (10 minutes)

- Introduce the topic of graffiti by asking students if they have ever read any graffiti which made them laugh, and to tell the class what it said. Ask students what makes graffiti like this funny or memorable (e.g. it says something that is wise or true, something that is unexpected, something that makes you stop and think).

- Write the following prompt for graffiti on the board: *If at first you don't succeed, …* and ask students, in pairs, to think of an ending for it.

- Have a class feedback session, then tell students the answer (*skydiving is not for you,* instead of the more usual *try, try again*).

Procedure (25 minutes)

- Explain that students are going to match halves of amusing graffiti quotations.

- Divide students into groups of ten and give each student two cards – the beginning of one graffiti quotation and the end of another one. (With larger classes, give each student one card only. With smaller classes, use fewer messages.) Give students a few minutes to read their half quotations, check any items of vocabulary, and memorize the text. Tell them to put the cards in their pocket as they are not allowed to read from them during the activity.

- When everybody is ready, ask students to mingle, telling each other their half quotations, until they find the person with the other half. When this happens, the student with the end of the quotation gives his/her card to the student with the beginning. Go around listening, checking that students are matching the quotations correctly.

- When everybody has finished, ask each student to read out his/her complete graffiti quotation. Check that everybody understands what it means. Ask students which quotation they thought was the funniest.

Note: If you would like to use all of the quotations with a small class, divide students into small groups. Give each group a set of cards. Students put the cards face up on the table and match the halves of the quotations.

Extension (5 minutes)

- Ask students, in small groups, to choose their favourite graffiti quotation and explain to the group why it appeals to them. Go around listening, helping with vocabulary as necessary.

Keep death off the roads!	Drive on the pavements instead.
'To do is to be' – Plato. 　　　'To be is to do' – Sartre.	'Do-be-do-be-do' – Sinatra.
Smile, they said, life could be worse.	So I did, and it was.
I used to be conceited,	but now I'm absolutely perfect.
I've half a mind to join the army …	That's all you need.
I used to be indecisive;	but now I'm not sure.
It's hard to make a comeback	when you haven't been anywhere.
I used to have a handle on life,	but it broke.
Passengers are requested 　　　not to cross the lines.	It takes hours 　　　to untangle them afterwards.
They came, they saw,	they did a little shopping.

7.2

To read strange, but true stories and speculate about possible explanations

Language

Modals for past possibility and certainty

Skills

Reading and Speaking

Lesson link

Use after Unit 7, SB p66

Materials

Two copies of the worksheet cut in half per group of four students

Answers

1 James Lews and James Springer are identical twins who were separated at birth. Each James married and divorced a woman named Linda. Each named his first son James. Both have the same hobbies and have had police training. They were 39 when they met for the first time.

2 In 1971, Edwin Robinson had a bad road accident and gradually lost his sight. One day, he went out for a walk with his guide dog, and was struck by lightning. He was unconscious for 20 minutes and when he came round, he could see again.

3 In 1975, a forestry worker called Travis Walton disappeared. He turned up five days later. He claimed he was abducted by aliens. He passed a lie-detector test.

4 Allison Burchell, 65, suffers from catalepsy (a sudden loss of muscular control) and has been pronounced dead three times. On one occasion, while nurses at a hospital prepared her for the morgue, she could hear them talking about their boyfriends. Later, she regained consciousness in the morgue and told a surprised nurse, 'I think you should leave your boyfriend.'

5 The next day the tree was cut down and a dart-riddled black bin liner was recovered.

Pre-activity (10 minutes)

- Read out or write the following situation on the board: *A woman returned to her apartment after a weekend trip to find another woman living there. The intruder, who was wearing her clothes, took her luggage and slammed the door in her face.*

- Explain that this is based on a true story, and ask students to speculate on what could/might/may/must/can't have caused the strange event, e.g. *She might have gone to the wrong house. The intruder must have been insane. The intruder can't have broken into the apartment; she must have had a key. She may have known the intruder. The intruder could have been her husband's ex-wife.* (Answer: The woman called the police, but the intruder insisted it was her apartment. She gave herself away when she misidentified the owner of the apartment building and said that John Wayne was taking her to dinner. She was detained for psychiatric tests.)

Procedure (30 minutes)

- Explain that students are going to read some strange stories and think about a plausible explanation for each. Tell students that the stories are all true stories.

- Divide students into groups of four and give each student a copy of the worksheet. (The text is reproduced twice on the worksheet for ease of copying.) Give students time to read the stories and to check any items of vocabulary.

- Ask students, in their groups, to speculate about what could/might/may/must/can't have happened in each situation. Remind them to use *must/can't have* with ideas they feel confident are correct, and *could/might/may have* with ideas they feel less confident about. Tell them to try and agree on the same explanation. Go around listening, helping and correcting as necessary.

- Have a class feedback session. Invite groups to tell the class what they thought, then tell students the correct explanation. Ask students which story they thought was the strangest / least believable / most frightening / funniest.

Extension (15 minutes)

- Ask students, in pairs, to write one of the stories as a newspaper article. Go around helping as necessary.

1 Two policemen met in Ohio. They had never met before and had no knowledge of each other, but they found out that their lives were identical.

2 It was raining when a man went out for a walk with his dog. During the walk he took shelter under a tree and lost consciousness. When he woke up his life had changed for the better.

3 A forestry worker saw a light in the woods while driving with five friends. He walked towards it, but was struck down by a flash. Terrified, the others drove away. Police tried to find him, but with no success. Five days later, he turned up in a nearby town.

4 While two nurses prepared a body for the morgue, they chatted about their boyfriends. Later when a nurse came back to move the body to a hospital ward, she was given some good advice.

5 A crowd of people tried to rescue a black bear up a twenty-metre tree. They used tranquiliser darts and nets, but the bear wouldn't come down. Finally, they cut down the tree, but the bear had disappeared.

---

1 Two policemen met in Ohio. They had never met before and had no knowledge of each other, but they found out that their lives were identical.

2 It was raining when a man went out for a walk with his dog. During the walk he took shelter under a tree and lost consciousness. When he woke up his life had changed for the better.

3 A forestry worker saw a light in the woods while driving with five friends. He walked towards it, but was struck down by a flash. Terrified, the others drove away. Police tried to find him, but with no success. Five days later, he turned up in a nearby town.

4 While two nurses prepared a body for the morgue, they chatted about their boyfriends. Later when a nurse came back to move the body to a hospital ward, she was given some good advice.

5 A crowd of people tried to rescue a black bear up a twenty-metre tree. They used tranquiliser darts and nets, but the bear wouldn't come down. Finally, they cut down the tree, but the bear had disappeared.

7.3

Two points of view

Aim
To discuss problem letters sent to an agony aunt and offer advice
Language
Giving advice
Skills
Reading and Speaking
Lesson link
Use after Unit 7, SB p68
Materials
One copy of the worksheet cut in half per group of four students

Pre-activity (5 minutes)

- Write *Problem page* on the board. Ask students where they can find them (in a women's magazine, in a tabloid newspaper). When did they last read a problem page? What type of problems do people usually have? (Possible answers: problems with work, with their partners, with their family, their home life, etc.) Do they think the advice given on problem pages is helpful?

- Quickly brainstorm different ways of giving advice, e.g. *Have you thought of / tried …? What you should/could do is …, Is there anything stopping you from …? It might be an idea to …, If I were you, I'd …, Your best bet is to …*, etc.

Procedure (25 minutes)

- Explain that students are the editors of a problem page in a weekly magazine called *Dear Judy*. They have received two letters and are going to decide on the best advice to give each person.

- Divide students into an even number of pairs: A and B. (If you have an odd numbers of pairs, make two groups of three.) Give Pairs A worksheet A, and Pairs B worksheet B.

- Give pairs time to read their letter, check any items of vocabulary, and discuss the advice they would give the person. Go around listening, helping with vocabulary as necessary.

- When students have finished, make groups of four with a Pair A and a Pair B. Pairs take it in turns to describe the problem in the letter they received and the advice they are going to give. Tell students they have to agree as a group on the advice for both letters and ask if they are tempted to change the advice they would give now that they know the situation from another point of view. (The letters are from a daughter and her mother both describing the same problem.)

- When groups have reached an agreement, have a class feedback session. Ask students what they think are the main pros and cons of living at home. Who do they sympathize most with: the mother or the daughter?

Extension (10 minutes)

- Ask students, in their original pairs, to write a reply to the letter they received. Remind them that these types of letter are informal, so they should reply using an informal style. Go around helping with vocabulary as necessary.

A

Dear Judy

Recently I've been having a few problems with my parents. They constantly interfere and comment on everything I do. I can't read a book or watch television without some remark. Whenever I go out, my mother wants to know exactly where I'm going and what time I'll be back. I wouldn't mind but I'm twenty-three years old!

My father is less worried about my social life and more concerned with my career. He's always going on about my job and whether I should consider a career change. At the moment I'm working for an aid organization and my salary is pretty low – in fact, I'm broke most of the time – but that's my problem. I just want to make a difference and he can't seem to understand that!

I've tried talking to my parents, but we just don't speak the same language. I can't afford a place of my own, but I can't carry on living at home – it's suffocating!

What should I do?

Holly

✂ -

B

Dear Judy

I'm writing to ask your advice about my twenty-three-year-old daughter. She's been living at home since she left university, and I'm starting to feel as if she is taking me, and her father, for granted. She comes and goes as she pleases, she doesn't help around the house – and she never listens to what we have to say.

At the moment, she's working for an aid organization and is paid a terrible salary considering her qualifications, but she doesn't seem to mind and is quite happy to carry on. Happy as long as we continue to support her, I suppose. Her father has talked to her about trying a different and more well-paid job, but she's not interested or even prepared to listen. We're trying to help, but she thinks we're interfering and tells us to mind our own business. That's very hurtful.

It seems like whatever suggestions we make, she always does the opposite. How can we get through to her?

Wendy Cooke

8.1

Going round in circles

Pre-activity (5 minutes)

- Write *heart*, *go*, and *storm* on the board. Give students, in pairs, two minutes to think of as many idioms as they can with these words (e.g. heart: *a heart of gold, lose heart, take heart*; go: *go round in circles, go down well, go to pieces*; storm: *take something by storm, weather the storm*).

- Have a class feedback session.

Procedure (25 minutes)

- Explain that students are going to play a card game making metaphors and idioms.

- Divide students into groups of three and give each group a set of cards, placed face down in a pile.

- Ask students each to take six cards but not to show them to anyone else in their group. Students leave the remaining cards in a pile on the table.

- Students take it in turns to play. If they have two cards which make a metaphor or an idiom, they can lay the cards face up on the table in front of them. For each card they lay down, they must pick up another from the pile. If they can't make any metaphors or idioms, they pick up one card from the pile. Go around checking and helping as necessary.

- In the following rounds, students lay down any new metaphors and idioms they can make.

- The game continues until all the cards have been used. The student who made the most metaphors and idioms is the winner.

Extension (10 minutes)

- Ask students, in pairs, to write five gapped sentences with some of the idioms and metaphors in the worksheet, e.g. *After a day on the mountain, Max was exhausted. Once he was in his sleeping bag, he was _____* (out like a light). Go around helping as necessary.

- Ask pairs to swap their sentences with another pair to complete.

take something to	heart	break someone's	heart
point the	finger	twist someone round your	finger
out like a	light	light	at the end of the tunnel
spark	someone's interest	a bright	spark
calm before the	storm	storm	in a teacup
to put down	root(s)	root(s)	of all my problems
go	round in circles	go	up in the world
reach	a crossroad in life	out of	reach

8.2

I wish ...

Aim	
To play a board game to talk about wishes and regrets or improbable situations	
Language	
Wishes and regrets	
Improbable situations	
Skills	
Speaking	
Lesson link	
Use after Unit 8, SB p78 & 79	
Materials	
One copy of the worksheet per group of four students. Each group will need a coin and each student will need a counter	

Pre-activity (10 minutes)

- Write the following prompts on the board and ask students, in pairs, to complete the sentences: *I wish my lifestyle ...*, *If there were no fast food restaurants ...* . Encourage them to be as creative as possible.

- When everybody has finished, ask pairs to read their sentences to the class.

Procedure (30 minutes)

- Explain that students are going to play a board game to talk about wishes and regrets or improbable situations.

- Divide students into groups of four and give each group a copy of the board game.

- Each student starts at a different corner on the board. Students take it in turns to toss a coin to move clockwise around the board (heads = move one square, tails = move two squares). When they land on a square, they complete the sentence and talk for a minute on that topic. If they dry up before this time, they have to move back one square. Go around listening, noting down any mistakes to go over later.

- The first student to get to the diagonally opposite corner on the board wins the game (i.e. A gets to C's start square).

Extension (10 minutes)

- Write any mistakes students have made on the board, and ask the class to correct them.

A	I wish the weather …	If I could visit any country …	I wish I didn't …	B
If there was a cure for …				If I was as rich as Bill Gates …
If animals could talk …				If I were a man/woman …
If only I could meet …				If TV hadn't been invented …
I wish there were …				If only cars were electric …
If we discovered life on another planet …				I wish my friends were …
If I could travel in time …				I wish I'd been …
If my mother tongue was international …				If there were holidays on the moon …
D	If I could choose any job …	If I was 15 years younger/older …	If only I could …	C

8.3

Picture this

Aim

To describe pictures and then write a dialogue

Language

Speculating

Wishes and regrets

Fluency practice

Skills

Speaking

Lesson link

Use after Unit 8, SB p78 & 79

Materials

One copy of the worksheet per group of four students

Pre-activity (5 minutes)

- Ask students if they have read the newspapers today. Ask if they have seen any interesting pictures in the papers. What were the pictures of and what were the stories about?

Procedure (25 minutes)

- Explain that students are going to look at some pictures and try and work out what is going on in each, before writing a dialogue to accompany one of the pictures.

- Divide students into groups of four and give each group a copy of the worksheet. Ask students to discuss what is happening in the pictures. What are the people in the pictures doing? How do they feel? What are they thinking? Do they have any regrets? What would students do in this situation? What advice would students give them? What do students think happened before this picture was taken? What happens next? Go around listening, helping with vocabulary as necessary.

- Have a class feedback session. Ask each group to tell you about one or two of the pictures.

- Divide students in each group into pairs. Ask students, in their pairs, to choose one picture and make a list of things they want to find out about the people and their situation, e.g. their names, their problems, the reason why they are there, what happened before the picture was taken, their wishes and regrets, what job they do, what happened after the picture was taken, etc.

- When students have finished their list, ask them to imagine the picture is taken from a film. Ask them to write a dialogue based on the picture, using their list to help them. Brainstorm ways of expressing regret with students, e.g. *I wish I hadn't done …, If only I wasn't …, Perhaps if I'd …, Maybe if you'd …,* etc. Students write their dialogue. Go around helping with vocabulary as necessary.

- When students have finished, ask pairs to act out their dialogue to the class. The listening students guess which picture it is based on. (If you have a large class, divide students into groups to act out their dialogues.)

Extension (10 minutes)

- Ask students, in pairs, to write a short caption for each of the other pictures. It could be something one of the people are saying or thinking, or it could be a sentence summing up the situation in the picture.

- Have a class feedback session and a vote for the best captions.

9.1

The same, but different

Aim

To play a game identifying words with the same spelling, but different pronunciation and meanings (homographs)

Language

Homographs

Giving definitions

Skills

Speaking

Lesson link

Use after Unit 9, SB p86

Materials

One copy of the worksheet cut up per group of four students

Start A			Start B
Finish B			Finish A

Pre-activity (5 minutes)

- If necessary, remind students that in English there are words which have the same spelling, but which are pronounced differently and have different meanings. These words are called homographs.
- Write the following sentence on the board: *I wound the bandage around the wound.* Ask students to identify the homographs and to tell you the pronunciation and meaning of the words (*wound* /waʊnd/ is the past of *wind* and means to put something around something, *wound* /wuːnd/ is an injury).

Procedure (25 minutes)

- Explain that students are going to play a game where they have to cross a board from one side to the other. In order to cross the board, they have to identify the homographs in a sentence, pronounce them correctly, and explain their different meanings.
- Divide students into groups of four, and each group into two teams: A and B. One team is noughts (O), the other is crosses (X).
- Draw the grid on the left on the board and ask each group to copy it onto a piece of paper.
- Explain that teams move from their start square to their finish square by winning squares and moving across the board. Tell them they can move up, down or to the side, but not diagonally.
- Give each group a set of cards placed face down on the table. Team A begins by picking up a card. They read out the sentence, pronouncing the homographs correctly, then explain the different meanings. If their pronunciation and definitions are correct, the team put a nought on a square on the grid, then play moves to the other team (who put a cross if they win a square). Once a square has a nought or cross, it cannot be used again. (Tell teams that they can choose squares to block their opponents as in a noughts and crosses game.) Go around helping and correcting as necessary.
- The team to cross the board first wins.

Extension (10 minutes)

- If necessary, remind students that in English there are words which have the same spelling and which are pronounced the same, but which have different meanings. These words are called homonyms.
- Ask students, in pairs, to write as many sentences as they can using the two meanings of the following homonyms from the Student's Book: *trunk, stern, branch, pine, deck, swallow, rare, rash, drill, scrap, rambling*, e.g. *The elephant picked up the trunk with his trunk. The captain gave me a stern look and as he walked towards the stern of the ship.* Go around helping as necessary.
- Ask pairs to read their sentences to the class.

The musicians took a week to record the record.

We were very content when he told us the content of his best man speech.

The farmer was asked to produce more produce.

She's standing at the bow of the ship wearing a bow in her hair.

It's my job to reject the reject machines.

What's the use of buying something you'll never use?

How often do you polish this Polish table?

The invalid man realized his car insurance was invalid.

The soldier decided to desert his post in the desert.

He was standing too close for me to close the door.

I think the present is a good time to present the prize.

There were tears in his eyes when he saw the tears in the painting.

I asked her to wind up the car window because of the wind.

They wanted to subject the subject to a day of tests.

We had a row at the cinema because I didn't want to sit in the front row.

He tried to intimate that the relationship was of an intimate nature.

After a number of injections my jaw got number.

I tried to console her when she started crying at the console.

I haven't read a good read for ages.

My boss spotted a minute mistake within a minute of reading my report.

9.2

Place your bets

Use after Unit 9, SB p88 & 89

Aim

To identify and correct grammatical mistakes

Language

Verb patterns

Skills

Speaking, Reading, and Writing

Lesson link

Use after Unit 9, SB p88 & 89

Materials

One copy of the worksheet per pair of students

Answers

1 Correct
2 The prisoner begged to be allowed another phone call.
3 Correct
4 My parents refused to buy me a motorbike.
5 Her postcard made him think about his last holiday.
6 Correct
7 Correct
8 Is it true that he's thinking of emigrating?
9 Correct
10 Luke suggested ordering a takeaway.
11 Clare's mum didn't stop her going out the night before her exam.
12 They dared him to try bungee jumping.
13 He threatened to tell the police if she didn't hand over the money.
14 The president wouldn't admit to having made a mistake.
15 Correct
16 He was trying to park his car when the accident happened.
17 Correct
18 Although he was exhausted, Mark carried on running.
19 Correct
20 Rachel regretted not going on holiday with us.

Pre-activity (5 minutes)

- Write the following sentences on the board:
    1 *Did you manage pass your driving test first time?*
    2 *I regret not telling the truth, but I really had no choice.*
    3 *She agreed working overtime at the weekend.*
- Give students, in pairs, two minutes to decide if the sentences are grammatically correct or not, and if not, to correct them.
- Have a class feedback session. Ask individual students to correct the sentences. (Sentence 2 is correct; *Did you manage **to pass** your driving test first time? She agreed **to work** overtime at the weekend.*)

Procedure (30 minutes)

- Explain that students are going to look at sentences, decide if they are grammatically correct or not, and correct the incorrect sentences. Tell students that they are also going to bet on how certain they are that the sentence is correct or that their correction is grammatically correct.
- Divide students into pairs and give each pair a copy of the worksheet. Give students twenty minutes to work through the sentences, correcting the incorrect ones and placing their bets in the boxes. Explain that each pair of students has €2,000 which they have to place as bets and they must bet on a minimum of fifteen sentences.
- Explain the betting rules to the students. If they bet correctly on a correct sentence, they get their original money back, plus the same sum again, e.g. bet €100, get €200 back, but if they also corrected the sentence, they get their original money back, plus double the money, e.g. bet €100, get €300 back. If they bet incorrectly, they lose the money they placed as a bet.
- Check the sentences with the class. Write the correct version on the board. Then give students a few moments to work out how much money they have won (or lost). The pair who won the most money wins.

This worksheet is based on an idea by Mario Rinvolucri.

Extension (10 minutes)

- Ask students, in pairs, to write five grammatically incorrect sentences. Go round helping as necessary.
- Ask pairs to swap sentences and correct each other's sentences. Go round checking and helping as necessary.

PLACE YOUR BETS

BET

1	She denied stealing money from the company.	
2	The prisoner begged allowed another phone call.	
3	He gave up making excuses and apologized.	
4	My parents refused buying me a motorbike.	
5	Her postcard made him thinking about his last holiday.	
6	My friends encouraged me to stop smoking.	
7	Kerry is used to getting her own way.	
8	Is it true that he's thinking to emigrate?	
9	They tried to stop the fire, but without much success.	
10	Luke suggested to order a takeaway.	
11	Clare's mum didn't stop her to go out the night before her exam.	
12	They dared him trying bungee jumping.	
13	He threatened telling the police if she didn't hand over the money.	
14	The president wouldn't admit to have made a mistake.	
15	Tanya's hairstyle was so strange that I couldn't help staring.	
16	He was trying parking his car when the accident happened.	
17	Don't worry – I remembered to lock the door.	
18	Although he was exhausted, Mark carried on to run.	
19	I wanted him to call me a taxi and take me home.	
20	Rachel regretted not to go on holiday with us.	

10.1

Aim
To define and discuss sports

Language
Fluency practice

Skills
Speaking

Lesson link
Use after Unit 10, SB p 92 & 93

Materials
One copy of the worksheet per student

Extreme ironing: competitors have to combine ironing with an extreme sport, e.g. climbing, white water rafting, diving. They carry an ironing board and iron to an extreme location and iron something.

Sky surfing: competitors have to jump out of a plane with a surfboard attached to their feet. The surfboard helps them do acrobatics or 'surf' the airwaves. It's a combination of sky diving and snowboarding.

Underwater hockey: two teams play against each other in a swimming pool. Each player wears a diving mask, a thick glove and has a wooden bat. The object of the game is to score goals. It's more or less the same game as hockey except that it's underwater.

Pre-activity (20 minutes)

- Write the following categories for Olympic sports on the board. Ask students to brainstorm more sports for each category.
  1. *races: relay, …* (100 m, 200 m, 400 m, 800 m, 1500 m, 5000 m, 10000 m, marathon, first three distances over hurdles, etc.)
  2. *measured events: long jump, …* (high jump, shot putt, discus, pole vault, triple jump, throwing the hammer, etc.)
  3. *contests: boxing, …* (judo, hockey, tennis, weight lifting, bowls, swimming events, etc.)
  4. *judged events: synchronized swimming …* (diving, figure skating, dressage, gymnastics – parallel bars, floor event, high bar, vaults, etc.)

- Write the following dictionary definition of sport on the board: ***sport** (n) a physical activity which is governed by objective rules and involves a contest or competition.* Ask students if all the sports they brainstormed conform to this definition. Ask if there are any which don't require a high level of fitness and athletic excellence, or if any are subjectively judged.

Procedure (30 minutes)

- Explain that students are members of the Olympic committee and that they have been asked to choose two new sports to be included in the next Olympic games.

- Divide students into groups of four and give each student a copy of the worksheet. Give students time to read the letter and look at the list of possible new sports. Explain *extreme ironing, sky surfing,* and *underwater hockey,* if necessary.

- Students discuss which two sports would be most appropriate to include in the Olympic games according to the criteria in the letter. Go around listening, helping as necessary.

- Have a class feedback session. Ask groups to tell the class their choice of sports, and to explain the reason for their choice.

Extension (10 minutes)

- Ask students if they agree with the definition of sport from the pre-activity. Ask students, in small groups, to write a new, more detailed definition of sport. Go around helping with vocabulary as necessary.

- Have a class feedback discussion.

International Olympic Committee

citius altius fortius swifter higher stronger

Dear Member

The International Olympic Committee is considering the addition of **two** new sports to the next Olympic Games. We need to come to an agreement about the most suitable sports to include, taking care that the new sports conform to most of the following Olympic criteria, i.e. competitive, skilful, artistic, objective, entertaining, a judged event, athletic, universal. Fulfilling most of these criteria is essential for selection as recently there has been a lot of debate about the nature of Olympic sport. The events put forward for consideration are listed below.

- snooker
- American football
- underwater hockey
- ballroom dancing

- extreme ironing
- computer games
- darts

- sky surfing
- bungee jumping
- sand skiing

I look forward to hearing from you.

Yours sincerely

President
International Olympic Committee

10.2

Aim

To write options for five questions and the personality profile for a personality quiz

Language

Character adjectives

Intensifying adverbs

Giving advice

Skills

Reading and Writing

Lesson link

Use after Unit 10, SB p94

Materials

One copy of the worksheet per pair of students. Each pair will need a sheet of paper

Possible answers

Mostly As: People usually enjoy being in your company because you are extremely confident and exciting. You love being the centre of attention and are a natural leader. You speak your mind, sometimes a little too freely.

Mostly Bs: You're a fun person and fairly confident. You speak your mind, but you're also quite sensitive and considerate to other people. Your friends like you because you're kind, interesting, and amusing. You're someone who'll cheer them up and help them out.

Mostly Cs: You're quite shy and careful. You're not very spontaneous and often think things through before you do something. You don't find it easy to make new friends, but once you know someone, you're very supportive and loyal. Sometimes you can be a bit unforgiving if someone lets you down.

Pre-activity (10 minutes)

- Brainstorm character adjectives with the class. Encourage students to supply intensifying adverbs which go with each adjective, e.g. *extremely self-confident, painfully shy, terribly bad-tempered*, etc.

- Ask students to imagine they have just arrived at a party. Would they: A) make a loud entrance so everyone knew they'd arrived, B) make a discreet entrance, then look around for a friend to talk to, or C) keep a very low profile and try to stay unnoticed?

- Ask students what type of person would choose options A, B, and C (A: extremely confident, an exhibitionist; B: quite confident, but also considerate; C: painfully shy and self-conscious).

Procedure (40 minutes)

- Explain that students are going to complete a half-written personality quiz for a magazine, and write a personality profile.

- Divide students into pairs and give each pair a copy of the worksheet and a sheet of paper. Give students time to read the quiz and to check any items of vocabulary.

- Ask pairs to write a personality profile based on the completed first half of the quiz on the sheet of paper, e.g. *Mostly As: You are someone …, Mostly Bs: People usually …, Mostly Cs: You are definitely …* . Encourage students to use the character adjectives and adverbs they brainstormed in the pre-activity and to give advice if necessary, e.g. *Maybe you should …, It'd be better if you …, Perhaps you ought to consider …, What about trying to …*, etc. Go around helping with vocabulary as necessary.

- Ask pairs to look at the prompts in questions 6–10 of the quiz and write the three options for each one, making sure options A–C conform to the personality profiles they wrote earlier.

- When everybody has finished, ask pairs to swap their quiz and personality profiles with another pair of students. Tell students not to look at the profiles yet.

- Students read the new quiz and individually note their answers for questions 1–10. Then they check their answers against the profile and decide if it accurately describes their personality.

Extension (10 minutes)

- Ask students to find the idioms and expressions with parts of the body in Questions 1–5 of the quiz (*put your foot down, put on a brave face, speak your mind, give someone the cold shoulder*).

- Ask students, in pairs, to write gapped sentences for the idioms and expressions, e.g. *John has _____ ever since I offended him at Rachel's party* (given me the cold shoulder). Go around helping as necessary.

- Students swap their sentences with another pair to complete.

PERSONALITY QUIZ

Personality quiz

Have you ever wondered how other people see you? Do this personality quiz and find out what kind of person you really are. Circle the answer which most closely matches what you do in each situation. Then read the profile for the letter (A, B, or C) you circled most often.

1 When you wake up in the morning, what do you do?

A Usually jump out of bed.

B Lie in bed for a few minutes, then get up.

C Turn on your side and go back to sleep.

2 You're having a disagreement with someone from work. What do you do?

A Put your foot down and stick to your point of view.

B Gradually back down and become off-hand about it.

C Put a brave face on it and give in.

3 When you enter the room at a party, what do you do?

A Go in and talk to the first person you see.

B Head straight for someone you recognize.

C Stand in the doorway and look round for someone you know.

4 You've had a serious argument with a friend. The next day they want to talk to you about it. What do you do?

A Speak your mind then leave without really listening to them.

B Sit down and calmly talk about it.

C Give them the cold shoulder and ignore them.

5 You meet someone for the second time and have forgotten their name. What do you do?

A Apologize and ask them to tell you.

B Wait and hope that their name will come up in conversation.

C Pretend that you haven't met them before.

6 What do you do to relax?

A _____

B _____

C _____

7 You're waiting in a queue and someone pushes in. What do you do?

A _____

B _____

C _____

8 When someone tells you a funny story, how do you respond?

A _____

B _____

C _____

9 You are overcharged for a meal in a restaurant. What do you do?

A _____

B _____

C _____

10 Someone interrupts you when you're concentrating on your work. How do you react?

A _____

B _____

C _____

10.3

Body language

Aim

To practise expressions with parts of the body words

Language

Expressions with parts of the body words in noun and verb form, e.g. *thumb a lift, be all fingers and thumbs*

Skills

Reading and Speaking

Lesson link

Use after Unit 9, SB p95

Materials

One copy of the worksheet cut up per group of four students. Groups will need a dictionary for the Extension

Answers

1 head
   A: totally, completely
   B: trying to achieve something, despite continually failing
2 shoulder
   A: ignore someone
   B: someone who listens to one's problems with sympathy
3 foot
   A: insist on doing something
   B: make a bad start
4 eye
   A: attract someone's attention
   B: have the same opinion
5 face
   A: show courage in times of difficulty
   B: meet criticism or punishment
6 elbow
   A: physical effort one puts into a task
   B: enough room to move freely
7 hand
   A: under control
   B: too casual
8 nose
   A: stay out of trouble
   B: pay more money for something than it's worth

Pre-activity (10 minutes)

- Brainstorm different parts of the body with the class. Then write these sentences on the board for students to complete with a body part:

   1   You shouldn't _____ a lift when you're travelling alone. Hitchhiking can be dangerous.

   2   Tom was all fingers and _____ with the baby. He had no idea how to hold her.

- Check the answer with the class (1 thumb; 2 thumbs). Then ask students if they can think of any other body parts which can be used as verbs, e.g. *head (a ball), foot (a bill),* etc.

Procedure (25 minutes)

- Explain that students are going to complete eight pairs of sentences. Each pair of sentences is missing the same body part. In the first sentence the body part is used as a verb, in the other it is part of an expression.

- Divide students into an equal number of pairs. (If you have an odd number of pairs, make two groups of three.) Give Pairs A worksheet A, and Pairs B worksheet B. Give students time to read their sentences, check any items of vocabulary and complete each gap with a body part. Go around helping as necessary.

- When students have finished, make groups of four with a Pair A and a Pair B. Explain that worksheets A and B have the same first sentences in each pair (i.e. those which use the body part as a verb), but different second sentences (i.e. those which use the body in an expression). Ask pairs to check that they have the same answers.

- Ask groups to discuss the meaning of the idiomatic expressions on the worksheets (the second sentence in each pair). Go around listening, helping as necessary.

- Have a class feedback session.

Extension (10 minutes)

- Using a dictionary, ask students, in small groups, to find another expression for each body part. Ask students to write sentences for each expression and gap the body part. Go around helping and correcting as necessary.

- Ask students to swap sentences with another group to complete.

A

1   The footballer couldn't _____ the ball into the net. He was too far away.

Simon thought Emma was wonderful. He was _____ over heels in love.

2   Kate had to _____ the responsibility of bringing up a child as well as earning a living.

Mark gave me the cold _____ and refused to speak to me last week.

3   At weddings, it's the bride's parents that usually _____ the bill.

Irene put her _____ down and refused to give in.

4   John shouldn't _____ up the girls all the time. His girlfriend gets terribly jealous.

The ring in the shop window caught his _____ . It was a perfect engagement ring.

5   You should _____ the facts. You're not going to get the job.

Despite feeling exhausted, Brett put on a brave _____ and finished the marathon.

6   It's rude to _____ someone out of the way. You should ask them politely to move.

Matthew put a lot of _____ grease into cleaning the car. It looked like new.

7   Sue volunteered to _____ out leaflets about the anti-war protest.

You don't need to help with the meal. Everything is in _____ .

8   You shouldn't _____ around the boss's office. You'll get into trouble if he finds out.

Ivan was told to keep his _____ clean by the police after they saw him writing graffiti on a wall near his school.

B

1   The footballer couldn't _____ the ball into the net. He was too far away.

She never listens to what I have to say. I feel like banging my _____ against a brick wall!

2   Kate had to _____ the responsibility of bringing up a child as well as earning a living.

Sue looks upset. I think she needs a _____ to cry on.

3   At weddings, it's the bride's parents that usually _____ the bill.

We definitely started the holiday off on the wrong _____ – we missed our flight!

4   John shouldn't _____ up the girls all the time. His girlfriend gets terribly jealous.

They don't see _____ to eye on many things. They're always arguing.

5   You should _____ the facts. You're not going to get the job.

Neil knew he had made a bad mistake. It was time to admit it and _____ the music.

6   It's rude to _____ someone out of the way. You should ask them politely to move.

There isn't enough _____ room at this table. The places are too close together.

7   Sue volunteered to _____ out leaflets about the anti-war protest.

Jerry was very off _____ about the exam. He wasn't taking it seriously at all.

8   You shouldn't _____ around the boss's office. You'll get into trouble if he finds out.

Rachel paid through the _____ for her new car. It was really expensive.

10.4

Aim
To find factual discrepancies between two newspaper stories

Language
Asking and answering questions

Skills
Reading, Speaking, and Listening

Lesson link
Use after Unit 10, SB p96

Materials
One copy of the worksheet cut up per group of three students

Pre-activity (5 minutes)

- Ask students about their favourite sports/film/pop stars. Ask them how often they read stories about them in the press. Ask if they always believe what is written. What type of publication is likely to be inaccurate or spread rumours and gossip? (Possible answers: tabloid newspapers, celebrity magazines.)

Procedure (30 minutes)

- Explain that students are going to interview a famous sports star to find out the fact and fiction in two newspaper articles.

- Divide students into groups of three. Give Students A worksheet A, Students B worksheet B, and Students C worksheet C. Tell students not to show each other their worksheets. Tell Students A and B that they are journalists, and Student C that he/she is Steve Striker, a famous footballer. Give students time to read their worksheets and to check any items of vocabulary.

- Tell Students A and B that they have to check the information in their newspaper story is correct by interviewing Striker. (You may like to pair Students A and Students B during this preparation stage.) Meanwhile Students C work through the questions on their worksheet and write additional notes for each question to build up the true story. Go around helping as necessary.

- When everybody is ready, Students A and B take turns to interview Student C. They make notes if they discover that any information in their newspaper story is incorrect. Go around listening, helping and correcting as necessary.

- After about ten minutes, ask students, in their groups, to look at both stories and decide which one was closer to the truth.

Extension (10 minutes)

- Ask students, in their groups of three, to write a factually correct newspaper story about Steve Striker. Encourage them to add any extra details from the interview to give their stories an exclusive feel, and to use intensifying adverbs to make their story more dramatic. Go round helping with vocabulary as necessary.

A

Bradchester United captain Steve Striker looked bitterly disappointed last night after his team's 1–0 defeat against Liverpool.

After the game, Striker is reported to have had a huge row with his coach, Max Fergal, who was completely infuriated by his poor performance. Steve left the changing rooms looking very upset, and refused to give a press interview. It's well-known that the two men really can't stand each other, and it looks as if Striker is ready to quit the team.

Striker's life off the pitch has been no better. Friends say he has become seriously addicted to gambling and has run up massive debts. Apparently there's not much left of the £2 million he earned last year. He is selling his mansion in Cheshire and is looking for a smaller property. His wife is said to be absolutely devastated and is threatening to leave him.

But it's not all bad news. Striker has recently been offered a hundred-thousand-pound contract with a top team in Italy. Because of his money problems, it's pretty certain he'll accept it.

B

Bradchester United captain Steve Striker is taking time off after losing 1–0 to Liverpool. Striker, usually quite brilliant, got injured and was taken off at half time.

Despite the defeat, coach Max Fergal is completely determined that the team will get through to the final of the championships. Fergal is keen for Striker to be totally fit by then.

Striker has had a very good year. He has earned over £3 million and he is looking to buy a second house in London. His wife, who absolutely adores him, is said to be pregnant with their second child.

But there's some worrying news for Bradchester United fans. Striker has been offered a multi-million-pound contract to play for an Italian team next season. It's rumoured that he won't accept it, but no one is quite sure yet.

C

You are the famous footballer Steve Striker, captain of Bradchester United. Your team have been losing recently and you are not playing in their next game. You are going to be interviewed by two journalists about your life. Look at the questions and decide what type of life you have. Write notes giving more information about each question.

- **Your coach Max Fergal:** Do you get on well or can't you stand him?
- **You are not playing in the next game:** Why? Have you got an injury or did you have an argument with your coach?
- **Earnings:** Did you earn £2 million or £3 million last year? Are you addicted to gambling?
- **Family life:** Does your wife absolutely adore you or is she ready to leave you? Is she pregnant?
- **Home:** Are you moving into a smaller house or are you buying a second house?
- **Work:** Have you been offered a contract with a new football team? How much? Are you going to accept it? Why? Why not?

11.1

Holiday clinic

Aim
To agree on the best holiday for a group of friends

Language
Suggesting
Agreeing and disagreeing

Skills
Speaking and Listening

Lesson link
Use after Unit 11, SB p100, 101, 102, & 103

Materials
One copy of the worksheet cut up per group of four students

Pre-activity (5 minutes)

- Brainstorm different types of holiday with the class (e.g. a cruise, beach holiday, package tour, independent travel, backpacking, trekking, adventure holidays, etc.).
- Ask students which types of holiday they prefer. Do they prefer to go on organized holidays or to travel independently? Do they like to stay in one place or move around?

Procedure (25 minutes)

- Explain that students are going away on holiday to Mexico with a group of friends and that they have to decide what type of holiday they want to go on.
- Divide students into groups of four and give each student a different role card: A, B, C, or D.
- Give students time to read their role card and to check any items of vocabulary. Students then take it in turns to tell the rest of the group about the holiday they would like.
- Give out the holiday section of the worksheet to each group. Ask students, in their groups, to read about the holidays on offer and discuss which one would best suit everybody in the group. Before students begin, brainstorm ways of making suggestions, accepting ideas, and raising objections, e.g. *Why don't we …?, What about + -ing?, What if we …?, That sounds like a great idea, It's definitely worth considering, I'm not keen on … because …, That might be OK, but …,* etc. Go around listening, helping as necessary.
- When everybody has finished, have a class feedback session. Ask each group to talk about the holiday they finally chose and the reason why they think it would suit everybody in the group. Ask students, if they had the choice, which holiday would they prefer to go on. You could have a class vote for the best holiday.

Extension (10 minutes)

- Ask students to imagine they are on holiday together in the place they agreed to go to. Ask them, in pairs, to write a postcard home describing a typical day, the group dynamics, and whether they are enjoying themselves. Go around helping with vocabulary as necessary.

Holiday Clinic

TEX MEX TOURS

from €450 per week (flights inc.)

Looking for fun in the sun? Look no further. Tex Mex tours have three-star hotels from only €450 per week. Price includes:

- return flights to Cancún
- full board at a three-star hotel
- day trip to Chichén Itzá
- organized games and theme evenings

Aztec APARTMENTS

from €450 per week
(flights not inc.)

Luxurious apartments just a stone's throw from the golden sands of Playa del Carmen. The apartments offer travellers a lot of independence while at the same time preserving the luxurious ambience of a five-star hotel. For more details and details of low-fare flights contact Aztec.

BUS MEXICO €150 for a three-week pass

Buy a discount three-week Linea Uno bus pass and travel all over Mexico. With your bus pass, you'll get a guidebook to Mexico's friendliest and cheapest hostels absolutely free. Perfect for people on the move and with a limited budget.

Mayan Experience

The Mayan Experience is committed to spreading the benefits of tourism more widely. Their guest houses are run by indigenous people and profits are used to help environmental programmes. We offer:

- reasonably-priced hostels along the Mayan route
- guided tours of archaeological sites and temple complexes
- visits to indigenous villages

from €275 per week
(discount flights €350)

Extreme Excursions

from €650 (plus return flights from €400)

Are you into extreme sports and tough, challenging adventure? Extreme Excursions offer adventure trips in remote areas of Chiapas for groups of three to twelve people.

- take a raft or canoe trip along the Lacanjà river
- camp out in hammocks in the Laguna Miramar jungle
- go caving near the Canyons of Rio La Venta

ECO RESORT

from €650
for two weeks
(flights not inc.)

For the ultimate Mexican escape come to Eco Paraiso. A small, exclusive hotel, Eco Paraiso is situated on a pristine beach on the edge of a nature reserve, teeming with wildlife. Our small hotel was constructed with great care to meet ecological standards. Guided tours around the mangroves are available.

A

You've been working hard recently and you feel you deserve a good break. You want to have a bit of luxury, and you've saved up some money. You like 'sun, sea, and sand' holidays where you can relax and have fun. You don't want to travel around.

B

You don't want to spend much on your holiday because you're saving up for your own flat. You're really interested in anthropology and learning about indigenous cultures. You like independent travel.

C

You're a bit of an adrenaline addict and very fit. As a result you like action-packed holidays where you can do some sort of sport or travel around a lot. You're currently learning Spanish and you want to have a lot of contact with local people so you can practise.

D

You're interested in wildlife and are a keen photographer. You'd prefer to spend time in one place so you can concentrate on your photography. You don't mind travelling a bit, but not every day. You usually take a lot of heavy photography equipment with you on holiday. Money is no problem for you.

11.2

Where in the world?

Aim

To describe and identify a holiday destination

Language

Compound nouns and adjectives to talk about the weather and places

Skills

Writing, Speaking, and Listening

Lesson link

Use after Unit 11, SB p104

Materials

One copy of the worksheet per pair of students

Answers

1 sun-baked, sunroof, suncream, sunburnt, sunstroke
2 snowstorm, snowflakes, snowdrift, snowbound, snowball
3 iceberg, ice falls, ice-bound, ice-free
4 raincoats, rain drops, rainfall, rain-soaked

Pre-activity (5 minutes)

- Write *sun*, *rain*, *ice*, and *snow* on the board. Ask students to brainstorm as many compound nouns and adjectives as they can, e.g. *sun-drenched*, *ice-cream*, *snow plough*, *rainfall*, etc. Write these as spider diagrams on the board, e.g.

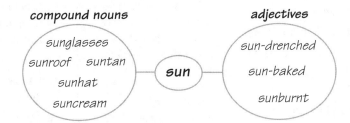

Procedure (25 minutes)

- Explain that students are going to read and complete extracts from four travel diaries, then write their own diary entry.

- Divide students into pairs and give each pair a copy of the worksheet. Give students time to read and complete the extracts with the words in the box.

- Check the answers with the class. Ask students where they think the people in the extracts are. How do they think they feel? Are they enjoying their stay?

- Ask students to imagine they are on holiday – it can be anywhere in the world – and write an extract from a travel diary, using compound nouns and adjectives with *sun*, *rain*, *ice*, and *snow*. Tell students to use as many of the compound words as possible and to gap the second word as in the extracts in the worksheet. Go around helping and correcting as necessary.

- When pairs have finished, ask them to swap their diary extracts with another pair to complete.

Extension (10 minutes)

- Ask students if they could go anywhere in the world, where would they like to go and why. Ask students, in small groups, to describe either their ideal destination or their nightmare destination. Go around listening, helping with vocabulary as necessary.

1

We drove for miles along the bottom of the sun-_____ valley with the sun _____ open. I didn't bother putting any sun _____ on, and when we arrived at the motel I noticed my forehead was terribly sun _____. Lucky I didn't get sun _____, really.

2

Spent today indoors. The weather forecast predicted a snow _____ this morning, so everything was closed down. Outside is just a swirl of snow _____ and there's already a big snow _____ blocking the door. It looks like the resort is going to be snow _____ for a few days – I suppose they'll be nothing to do but have snow _____ fights!

3

We passed an ice _____ this morning. It was quite spectacular – you could clearly see the ice _____ on one side. We arrived at the port around 4 pm. Apparently we are the first to visit. It's usually ice-_____ at this time of year, but it's been ice-_____ for weeks – global warming, I suppose.

4

Funny weather at the moment - not what we expected at all, and we haven't even brought our rain _____. Went for a walk today - there were a few rain _____ when we started out, but the sky looked as if it was going to clear. Unfortunately, that didn't happen. After half an hour we got caught in torrential rain _____. By the time we got back we were completely rain-_____ - to make matters worse I think I'm getting a cold!

baked	ball	berg	bound	bound	burnt	coats	cream	drift
drops	fall	falls	flakes	free	roof	soaked	storm	stroke

11.3

A tale of two cities

Answers

1 h After deciding to go away for a few weeks, Emma and Raoul looked on a holiday website.
2 l While searching the site, they found a cheap flight to Sydney via Canada.
3 b By flying via Canada, they would save a lot of money.
4 j Not having been to Sydney before, they decided to book it.
5 e Five days after buying their tickets, they were on the plane.
6 g After landing in Halifax, Canada, they went to board the next plane.
7 c While checking in for their flight, they noticed that the plane was very small.
8 d Not thinking the plane was big enough to fly to Australia, they checked the destination – it was Sydney.
9 f After flying for forty-five minutes, the pilot announced they were landing in Sydney.
10 i On looking out of the window, they realized their mistake.
11 a Not realizing there were two Sydneys, they'd booked a holiday in Sydney, Nova Scotia!
12 k Not having a hope of reaching Sydney, Australia, the couple had to stay.

Pre-activity (5 minutes)

- Ask students if they have ever booked a holiday or a flight on the Internet. Ask them what the advantages are of booking a flight on the Internet. Is it easy to do? Is it easy to make a mistake?

- Write the following sentences on the board: *I saw a flight. I was searching a travel website. I booked the flight on the Internet so I got a 20% discount.* Ask students to rewrite them using present participles. (*While searching a travel website, I saw a flight. By booking the flight on the Internet, I got a 20% discount.*) Check the answers with the class.

Procedure (25 minutes)

- Explain that students are going to rewrite some sentences from a true story using present participles.

- Divide students into an even number of pairs: A and B. (If you have an odd numbers of pairs, make two groups of three.) Give Pairs A worksheet A, and Pairs B worksheet B.

- Explain that the sentences of the story are not in order and that each pair has only half of the story at the moment. Give pairs time to rewrite the sentences using present participles. Go around helping and correcting as necessary.

- When students have finished, make groups of four with a Pair A and a Pair B. Ask students to check each other's sentences and put the story in order. Go around checking and helping as necessary.

- Ask groups to read the ordered story together and decide where using the participle phrase sentences helps the story, making it sound more natural. In the other places, ask students to replace the participles with a relative or conjunction, e.g. *When they looked out of the window, they realized their mistake.* Encourage them to read the story aloud to hear the different effects of the various choice of structures. Go around helping as necessary.

- Have a class feedback session. Ask students how easy a mistake this was to make. Could they imagine making the same mistake?

Extension (10 minutes)

- Ask students how the participles are used in each sentence. Write these alternatives on the board for them to match with the participles in the story: *used when two events happen at the same time* (c, l), *used to introduce a reason* (a, d, j, k), *used to introduce a result* (b, i), *used when one event happens after another* (e, f, g, h).

A

a They hadn't realized there were two Sydneys. They'd booked a holiday in Sydney, Nova Scotia!
   Not ...

b If they flew via Canada, they would save a lot of money.
   By ...

c They checked in for their flight and noticed that the plane was very small.
   While ...

d They thought the plane wasn't big enough to fly to Australia so they checked the destination – it was Sydney.
   Not ...

e They were on the plane five days after they had bought their tickets.
   Five days after ...

f Forty-five minutes into the flight, the pilot announced they were landing in Sydney.
   After ...

✂ -

B

g They landed in Halifax, Canada. They went to board the next plane.
   After ...

h Emma and Raoul decided to go away for a few weeks. They looked on a holiday website.
   After ...

i They looked out of the window and realized their mistake.
   On ...

j They hadn't been to Sydney before so they decided to book it.
   Not ...

k They didn't have a hope of reaching Sydney, Australia, so the couple had to stay.
   Not ...

l They searched the website and found a cheap flight to Sydney via Canada.
   While ...

12.1

Aim

To complete sentences with expressions with *time*, then make a chain with the sentences

Language

Expressions with *time*

Fluency practice

Skills

Writing, Speaking, and Reading

Lesson link

Use after Unit 12, SB p110 & 111

Materials

One copy of the worksheet per pair of students and pairs of scissors

Possible answers

We've got time to kill because ... the film doesn't start for another hour.

Only time would tell whether I ... had made the right decision.

Ella arrived in the nick of time just as ... the train was about to leave.

Helen is difficult at the best of times ... but this time she was just plain rude.

I decided to bide my time and ... wait for the right moment to ask for a promotion.

I was a bit pressed for time so ... I got a taxi into town.

You've got to move with the times if ... you want to get on in the world of big business.

The lawyer bought some time by ... delaying the trial.

It's about time you ... left, otherwise you'll miss your flight.

I can't believe how time flies ... when you are enjoying yourself.

I met up with him for old time's sake although ... we had nothing in common.

Pre-activity (5 minutes)

- Write *People are really behind the times if ...* on the board and elicit a possible ending to the sentence, e.g. *they don't have a mobile phone.*

- Ask students, in pairs, to think of other possible endings to the sentence. Encourage students to be creative. Then have a class feedback session.

Procedure (25 minutes)

- Explain that students are going to complete sentences with expressions with *time*, then make a chain with the sentences.

- Divide students into pairs and give each pair a copy of the worksheet. Show students how to complete each sentence by writing in the blank space on the card underneath it, e.g. students write the completion of *We've got time to kill because ...* in the blank section by *Only time would tell whether I ...*, etc. (The completion of *I met up with him for old time's sake although ...* is written in the blank section by *We've got time to kill because ... .*)

- Go around helping and correcting as necessary, checking that the sentences make sense.

- When everybody has finished, give each pair of students a pair of scissors and ask them to cut up the cards following the dotted lines. Make sure they don't cut down the solid line in the middle.

- Ask pairs to swap their cards with another pair. Pairs look at their new cards and try to match them to make sentences. Tell students to put the cards in a circle as a way to check they have matched them correctly. Go around helping as necessary.

- When students have finished, ask the pairs who wrote the sentence completions to check that the cards have been matched correctly.

Extension (10 minutes)

- Ask students, in pairs, to choose four expressions with *time* from the worksheet and to write definitions for them. Students swap their definitions with another pair, who match them to the expressions in the sentences.

- Have a class feedback session. The class can decide on the best definitions.

We've got time to kill because …

Only time would tell whether I …

Ella arrived in the nick of time just as …

Helen is difficult at the best of times …

I decided to bide my time and …

I was a bit pressed for time so …

You've got to move with the times if …

The lawyer bought some time by …

It's about time you …

I can't believe how time flies …

I met up with him for old time's sake although …

12.2

Time capsule

Aim

To select the contents for a time capsule

Language

Making suggestions

Giving reasons

Skills

Reading, Listening, and Speaking

Lesson link

Use after Unit 12, SB p114

Materials

One copy of the worksheet cut in half per two students

Pre-activity (10 minutes)

- Write *Time capsule* on the board. Ask students what the purpose of a time capsule is and if they know of any famous time capsules, e.g. NASA time capsules, Cleopatra's needle time capsule. What type of things do people put in them? Ask students to imagine they have found a time capsule in their area from 1920. What would they expect or hope to find inside?

Procedure (25 minutes)

- Explain that the technology now exists to send things back in time and that students are going to choose things to put into a time capsule to be sent back to the 1970s. Have a quick discussion about the types of things students might like to include in the time capsule. Revise phrases for making suggestions and giving reasons during this discussion, e.g. *We should really include … so as to …, Why don't we …? Couldn't we … in order to …? That way people can …, It'd be a good idea to … so that …,* etc.

- Divide students into groups of two to four and give each student a copy of the worksheet. (The text is reproduced twice on the worksheet for ease of copying.) Give students time to read the worksheet and to check any items of vocabulary.

- Ask students, in their groups, to think of five more things to add to the list. Remind students that the capsule is small so they shouldn't add anything large. Go around listening, helping with vocabulary as necessary.

- Have a quick class feedback session to see what things the groups have added. Then ask students to discuss which they think are the five most important things to put into the time capsule. Tell students to give reasons for their choice each time they make a suggestion to the group.

- Have a class feedback session. Ask groups to tell the class their choice of items and their reasons for choosing them. Can the class agree as a whole on which five items to include?

Extension (10 minutes)

- Ask students, in their groups, to write a letter to go with their time capsule, explaining the main changes in everyday life since the 1970s. They should explain what the different objects in the capsule are used for, especially technical items which won't be able to work in the 1970s, e.g. CDs, ATM cards, mobile phones.

Technololgy Today

Dear _____

Congratulations! You have won this month's Time Travel competition. Your prize is to choose **five items** to go into a time capsule. As you know, scientists have recently made an exciting breakthrough in time travel. They are now able to send small, simple objects back in time. As a result, they have decided to send a time capsule back to the 1970s. The aim of the project is to give scientists in the '70s a flavour of everyday life at the beginning of the twenty-first century. The capsule is quite small so there won't be room for things like DVD players, TVs, or computers. Researchers have also made a list of possible items (please see below). Please feel free to make your selection from this list, or to add and choose from your own ideas.

Look forward to hearing from you soon.

Yours sincerely

Pat Ransdall

Pat Ransdall
Editor, Technology Today Magazine

☐ a mobile phone ☐ decaffeinated coffee ☐ _____
☐ a TV remote control ☐ a product with a bar code ☐ _____
☐ mineral water ☐ an ATM card ☐ _____
☐ recycled packaging ☐ an MP3 player ☐ _____
☐ anti-depressants ☐ a hand-held computer ☐ _____

✂ -

Technololgy Today

Dear _____

Congratulations! You have won this month's Time Travel competition. Your prize is to choose **five items** to go into a time capsule. As you know, scientists have recently made an exciting breakthrough in time travel. They are now able to send small, simple objects back in time. As a result, they have decided to send a time capsule back to the 1970s. The aim of the project is to give scientists in the '70s a flavour of everyday life at the beginning of the twenty-first century. The capsule is quite small so there won't be room for things like DVD players, TVs, or computers. Researchers have also made a list of possible items (please see below). Please feel free to make your selection from this list, or to add and choose from your own ideas.

Look forward to hearing from you soon.

Yours sincerely

Pat Ransdall

Pat Ransdall
Editor, Technology Today Magazine

☐ a mobile phone ☐ decaffeinated coffee ☐ _____
☐ a TV remote control ☐ a product with a bar code ☐ _____
☐ mineral water ☐ an ATM card ☐ _____
☐ recycled packaging ☐ an MP3 player ☐ _____
☐ anti-depressants ☐ a hand-held computer ☐ _____

12.3

Race against time! 2

Aim

To do a quiz to revise grammar and vocabulary from Units 7–12

Language

Grammar and vocabulary review

Skills

Reading

Lesson link

Use after Unit 12

Materials

One copy of the worksheet per pair of students. A bag of sweets or similar for a prize

Answers
Grammar

1. would have
2. to climb
3. seriously/really/actually/honestly
4. must have finished
5. seemed to be getting better …
6. I really can't stand Mike.
7. served
8. Having witnessed / After witnessing
9. absolutely
10. see them
11. unless, if
12. After reading my book, I turned out the light.
13. On finding a bag of money, he called the police.
14. That's the friend whose sister I've been working with.
15. He tiptoed up the stairs so as not to wake the children.
16. real

Pre-activity (5 minutes)

- Ask students if they are confident that they can remember all the grammar and new vocabulary from Units 7–12. Elicit some of the areas covered with the class.

- Write the following sentences on the board for students to complete and correct:

  1 *They _____ arrived yet. They only left a few minutes ago.*

  2 *Is the door open? I can feel a draft.*

- Check the answers with the class (1 can't have, 2 draught).

Procedure (30 minutes)

- Explain that students are going to do a quiz which tests the grammar and vocabulary from Units 7–12. They have ten minutes to do as many questions as they can.

- Divide students into pairs and give each pair a copy of the worksheet placed face down on the table.

- Shout: *Start!* Pairs turn over the worksheet and start working through the quiz. Go around monitoring but not helping at this stage.

- Stop the activity after ten minutes. Ask pairs to swap their worksheets with another pair for marking. Go through the answers with the class.

- The pair with the most correct answers wins. (It is a good idea to have a prize, e.g. a bag of sweets, for the winning pair.)

Extension (10 minutes)

- Ask students, in their pairs, to write two more grammar and vocabulary questions for another pair to answer. Go around helping as necessary.

Answers
Vocabulary

1. up-to-date, current
2. world
3. point the finger, take your breath away, a few hiccups, etc.
4. shoulder
5. hands
6. fingers
7. snow (x3)
8. impartial, open-minded, liberal
9. trivial, irrelevant, unimportant
10. to pass away
11. After the marathon, my legs felt tired and sore.
12. He drove a cheap, rusty, red, convertible car.
13. They bought a dusty, cut-price, Chinese vase from the antique shop.
14. I wonder if / Could you possibly pass me the magazine?
15. (suggestion) Looking out of the window as we flew over the Sahara, all I could see was windswept sand dunes for miles and miles.
16. (suggestion) Despite their stormy relationship, they stayed together and tried to work our their differences.

RACE AGAINST TIME!

10 | 9 | 8 | 7 | 6 | 5 | 4 | 3 | 2 | 1

Grammar

Complete the sentences.

1 None of this _____ happened if you'd been paying attention!

2 Although it was risky, she attempted _____ the rock face.

3 Do you _____ believe that we can win?

Correct the mistakes.

4 They must have been finished by now. They've been working for hours.

5 The weather seemed getting better as we drove south.

6 I completely can't stand Mike. He just gets on my nerves.

7 Steak is excellent when serving with a red wine sauce.

8 Witnessing the accident, we quickly called the emergency services.

Choose the correct alternative.

9 It is *absolutely / totally* essential that you pack your parachute carefully.

10 Did you *see them / mind them* arrive late?

11 We could meet at the station *providing / unless* my train is cancelled. I'll give you a call *providing / if* there are any problems.

Rewrite the sentences.

12 I read my book. I turned out the light.
After _____

13 He found a bag of money. He called the police.
On _____

Combine the sentences.

14 That's the friend. I've been working with her sister.
_____

15 He tiptoed up the stairs. He didn't want to wake the children. (so as not to)
_____

Answer the question.

16 Is this an example of real or unreal tense usage?
He was convinced they'd met before, but he couldn't remember where.

Vocabulary

Complete the sentences.

1 Two synonyms for *modern* are _____ and _____ .

2 A homophone for *whirled* is _____ .

3 Two metaphors to do with the body are _____ and
_____ .

4 Mark had to _____ the responsibility of supporting his family from a very early age.

5 You *frisk* someone with your _____ .

6 You *tickle* someone with your _____ .

7 After the _____ storm it took ages for the _____ plough to get through to the village. There were huge _____ drifts blocking the roads.

8 Two antonyms for *prejudiced* are _____ and _____ .

9 Two synonyms for *petty* are _____ and
_____ .

10 A euphemism for *to die* is _____ .

Correct the mistakes.

11 After the marathon, my legs felt tired and soar.

12 He drove a convertible, rusty, cheap, red, car.

13 They bought a Chinese, dusty, cut-price, vase from the antique shop.

Write sentences.

14 Make this request more tactful: *Pass me the magazine.*

15 Make a sentence with a compound noun with *wind.*

16 Make a sentence with a metaphor using the word *stormy.*

10 | 9 | 8 | 7 | 6 | 5 | 4 | 3 | 2 | 1 | TIME'S UP!